RHIANNON SPURGEON prides herse
to even the darkest clouds, and rarely los
Creating positive ripples in her everyday
they brighten one person's day or impact a

She is the founder and head cheerleader at the Totally Awesome Women's Network, manages an enterprise hub, coaches, mentors and writes. The earlier years of her career featured stints at the House of Commons, *Financial Times* and The Prince's Trust. Widowed with a ten-day-old baby at the age of 34, Rhiannon has spent the last ten years as a working single mum, putting down roots and keeping all the plates spinning.

'Face everything and recover' is her personal motto. She loves her family and friends, dogs, dancing, creating, laughter, taekwondo and her sobriety.

Grief Without Guilt is her first book.

GRIEF WITHOUT GUILT

It Gets Better If You Let It,
Even If It's Complicated

RHIANNON SPURGEON

To dea Kate
That you fo all of ya
sypot, ₰ with love
SilverWood
Rhianne
L.

Published in 2021 by SilverWood Books

SilverWood Books Ltd
14 Small Street, Bristol, BS1 1DE, United Kingdom
www.silverwoodbooks.co.uk

ISBN 978-1-80042-077-9 (paperback)
ISBN 978-1-80042-078-6 (ebook)

British Library Cataloguing in Publication Data
A CIP catalogue record for this book is
available from the British Library

Page design and typesetting by SilverWood Books

GRIEF WITHOUT GUILT

For Oliver,
in gratitude for everything good in my life

Our life was far from perfect
And then he went and died
Nobody understood what happened
So, my story felt like lies

I wasn't there when it happened
And our last words weren't "I love you"
He'd asked me and I had said "yes"
But we never did "I do"

We had some days of better
And many days of worse
Our last words weren't "I love you"
And he left me in a hearse

Our last words weren't "I love you"
And we never said goodbye
He was so far from perfect
But I will miss him 'til I die

Words escaped that shouldn't have
And others remained unsaid
I wish I'd said "I love you"
One more time, but now you're dead.

31.10.19

Contents

Introduction

"If you're going through hell, keep going"
(source unknown)

You can be okay.

It may not feel like it right now, but you can be okay.

Your track record for getting through tough days so far is 100%, you can be okay.

No matter how lonely you feel right now, you are not alone.

You are not the only person who feels stuck.

You are not the only one who knows what it feels like to not have a simple explanation.

You are not the only one who sums it up with "It's complicated".

You are not the only one for whom the last words weren't "I love you".

You are not the only one feeling little rushes of relief that some elements of your story are over.

You are not the only one feeling guilty about those little rushes of relief.

You can be okay.

This is the book that I needed when it happened to me. This is the book that I wish had been written by somebody else ten years earlier, so that it existed when I needed it.

When Oliver died, I had nobody I could *really* talk to. I didn't want platitudes. I didn't even really want anyone walking in silence beside me as I ranted or cried, as much as I appreciated the people who were willing to do that.

I wanted to know that somebody else had been in this dark, lonely and confusing place that I now inhabited, and that they'd survived and got out and that the lights had come back on.

I wanted to know that I wasn't just going to spend the rest of my life in this relentless void.

I wanted to know that I would live again, outside of the shadows.

I wanted to know that I could be happy.

I wanted to know that I could laugh without feeling that I shouldn't.

I wanted to know that I could be free.

I wanted to know that it would get better.

But nobody told me these things or, if they did, I didn't hear them.

There are people in our lives who want us to get better. We know they want us to get better. It can be hard to see how they can help though.

Because they don't feel what we feel.

The people who love us and the professionals who are paid to care for us cannot possibly *know* that we can get better because they haven't *been* here, they haven't felt this way. If they haven't been in this place, haven't felt the crippling guilt that maybe, just maybe, the person you loved, no matter how fucked up that love was, might be dead because of something you did or did not do or say, then they cannot know.

But I have, and now I am offering to share my story with you, so that you do not feel so alone.

As I finish writing this book, Oliver has been gone for nine years. While losing him prompted me to write, he wasn't the first. When I was a teenager, I met and loved and lost a boy, and I was quite sure it was my fault. I have twenty-five years of personal experience in this field.

Bereavement Counselling

I have had help from professionals over the years, but I've never been to bereavement counselling.

My doctor gave me a phone number to call to connect with a bereavement counsellor when the news of Oliver's death was fresh. A few weeks later, she reminded me and offered me the number again. I never called it. Years down the line, I still haven't made that call.

If you have, I hope it helped. If you haven't, maybe me sharing my story will help to explain why I didn't seek that kind of support.

I had this image of what a bereavement counsellor would look and smell like. She would be some terribly kind middle-class lady in her 60s, with a selection of smart cardigans and a vague smell of those Elizabeth Arden perfumes they sell in independent chemists. She would be more used to comforting widows of a more traditional age and background who had lost their life partner of twenty, thirty or forty years. Or maybe she would have experience dealing with cancer families, or car accident deaths, or even murders.

But I couldn't envisage her being a person who could help *me*.

My story was messy and complicated and would inevitably be littered with swear words and I just couldn't see how that kind middle-aged lady could help me with that.

I judged this person that I'd never even called in the same way I feared she would judge me.

And then there was time. Our baby girl was ten days old when Oliver died, and her incessant needs were my highest priority. They were, in the main, my *only* priority. She was the reason I got out of bed. Feeding her was the only reason I ate food. For quite some time, she was my central and only reason for living. If counselling meant time away from her, and if I couldn't see counselling being of direct and immediate benefit to her, it just wasn't a good use of my time.

So, I didn't go.

When things settled a bit, I thought I'd sound like a fraud if I called up months after the event. In my head, bereavement counsellors were there for people in the initial throes of shock and disbelief.

Sometimes, I wonder if making that call might have made a difference to how dark the shadows were, or how long I lived within them. But I will never know because it was not the path I chose.

The Power of Sharing Your Truth

Now, of course, I know how powerful it can be to connect with somebody who understands the messiness and the guilt. Meeting and connecting with Ben changed so much for me.

It took me five years to meet somebody who I could really share my story with. Ben is the father of one of my daughter's school friends and he is a widower. When I met him, he was not in a good place. He was raising two daughters by himself, had the pallor of a nightcrawler and rarely left the house other than to walk to and from his daughters' school.

I wish I could remember how the conversation started. I remember we were in his living room, and the shrine to his late wife covered an entire wall. I asked about her, and he opened up a bit. I shared some of my 'it was less than perfect' and he shared some of his. We talked and listened to each other and, for three or four hours that night, we both let go of stuff, while our daughters played in the next room.

Afterwards, I felt lighter.

I felt heard and, most importantly, I didn't feel judged. I had shared my truth and I was okay.

Ben and I have little else in common, but I will be forever grateful for that evening. Being heard and understood by somebody who knew what it was like to have had a messy relationship that ended with a messy death was invaluable.

I can't speak for Ben or whether that conversation had the same impact on him, but he now has a new partner, looks healthy and smiles a lot more than he used to.

This Book

This book is my way of inviting you to open up and let go of what is holding you back. This is a safe space.

In the following chapters, I will share with you the stages that I moved through, offering some practical advice and, at the end of each chapter, some journal prompts. There is also an online community you can join if you would like to share your story with other people who get it.

I have included some of my poems in the section breaks. Some were written on specific anniversaries and are dated; others were written over a period of years and I can't remember exactly when I finished them. Writing poetry helped me to figure out my feelings and gave me a way to express them without needing to explain myself. I have written poems like these over the years and have found them therapeutic. When I have shared them on social media, they have also presented my friends with a way to say "Thinking of you" and "Love you" without having to struggle to find more words. Their entire meanings and the images they recall remain mine alone, but if you gain comfort from or find meaning in them, then I am glad to have included them.

Writing my story has helped with my healing process and

I hope that sharing my story will help you with yours.

In essence, there is a pathway through grief. While it will look different for each one of us, we can all find it if we look for it. Before I started writing this book, and what I went through again several times throughout the process, looked a bit like this:

1. Own your story
2. Process what you've lost, and gained
3. Let go of what is holding you back
4. Embrace your freedom
5. Find strength in vulnerability
6. Encourage others to share their stories with you

I'll return later to the topic of how sequences and deadlines can be overwhelming and misleading. This is just *my* way of doing it. I'm hoping that by showing up and laying myself bare, you'll find some sense of solidarity.

You are not walking this path alone.

Your path may look very different from mine, and that's okay, as long as you're moving through the dark forest instead of going in circles and just getting tired.

There is no one-size-fits-all in life, death or grief.

And just because I've not yet been to a bereavement counsellor doesn't mean I never will. A friend who is a bereavement counsellor has told me that a lot of people reach out a year or two after their person has moved on to the next place. Bereavement counsellors are not just there for the immediate aftermath of a death. If you want to reach out for help, at whatever stage and no matter how long you've been bereaved, then do. There are a lot of qualified people who can listen without judgement, and that may be exactly what you need.

It gets better if you let it. xx

Part One

Own Your Story

The man I love I cannot have
"Is he married?"
"Is he gay?"
"No, no, no he's dead," I say

His battles fought,
Some even won
The wreckage cleared,
The filing done

Most loose ends tied.
I hope you found
the peace you sought
on the night
you died.

"It's Complicated"

"It's complicated". Those two words can shut down a conversation or pique curiosity.

Do they resonate with you?

When I was young and thought that drama made me interesting, I used to use those words as a prelude to a story. As I got older and my perspective changed, I used them to avoid having to tell one.

What do they mean for you?

There are many incarnations of the complicated relationship, and most of the people in those relationships don't want to be asked how it works. In life, being in a relationship that can only be put into the 'it's complicated' box can be challenging enough. When one of the people in that relationship dies, "it's complicated" can reach a whole new level of tough.

For me, "it's complicated" covers our seven year on-off-friends-lovers relationship, addiction, his family, the other women in his life, legal issues and a death that had its own inquest.

For other people, it's different. It could mean that you were having an affair with the person who died. It might have been a torrid and passionate fling, or it might have been more of a Charles and Camilla star-crossed soulmates situation.

You might have been the same sex partner of somebody who was publicly heterosexual and even married with children.

It might be that you'd broken up with the person years earlier and, therefore, feel no 'right' to grieve.

You might have been desperately unhappy in the relationship, or even abused in it, and your support circle cannot understand your grief.

You might even be the person who feels responsible for somebody ending their life. Or the person who others blame for it.

You might have been the one who knew that person best in the world, but that didn't protect you from feeling excluded when they died.

Relief and Guilt

I wasn't there when Oliver died. I had issued him an ultimatum about going to rehab. Professional advice said that if I went back on it, I was condemning him to die of his alcoholism. I loved him, so I followed their advice and remained silent. I couldn't undo the last thing I'd said to him. I couldn't turn it into "I love you", precisely because I loved him.

I went through the final trimester of pregnancy and the birth of our daughter without him, because I loved him. On my darkest days, I felt quite sure that he'd died because I loved him.

Of course, he'd told me many times in the last year and a

half that we were together that he was only alive because of me. Sometimes he got grumpy with me because I wouldn't give up on him.

And, still, I blamed myself for his death.

Almost worse, I felt relieved that some parts of my life were now over.

But every glimmer of relief was swiftly followed by guilt. How on earth could I feel relieved about any of it?

I was never relieved that he was dead. I loved him, every fucking broken angry needy bit of him. But the life we led together was no fairy tale.

He desperately wanted children and, on his good days, we would joke about having four. We both knew he wouldn't be able to be the dad he'd always wanted to be. His body wouldn't let him. He wanted to hold our babies up like Rafiki holds Simba in *The Lion King*, but we both knew he wouldn't be able to. He wanted to be the fun dad he'd always wished he'd had, but we both knew he wouldn't be able to. Even if his mind had been healed, his body was irreparably broken.

I was relieved I would never have to watch his heart break as he acknowledged all the things he couldn't do.

I was relieved I wouldn't have to reassure him that he wasn't failing as a dad because he couldn't do the things that his disability precluded him from.

I was relieved that I wouldn't have to spin all the plates of being the breadwinner, the parent and the carer.

I was relieved that I would no longer have to schedule my life around hospital appointments.

I was relieved that I would no longer have to be hyper vigilant about his ex-girlfriends or the nightmare neighbour.

I was relieved that I wouldn't have to apologise for his bizarre behaviour when he hallucinated or embarked on one of his sleepwalking expeditions.

I was relieved that I wouldn't have to live in fear of the police turning up on the doorstep yet again to topple the delicate balance of our lives.

I was relieved about the stressful and draining things that I would no longer have to accommodate in my life. And, before I'd even exhaled that breath, I was hit by the wave of guilt. How could I be so selfish? How could I possibly look at my life now as *easier*? That is a specific type of guilt that any of us can so easily drown in if we choose to.

Dealing with the endless stress had robbed me of much of the joy I should have felt in my pregnancy. I lived in fear that my baby would be damaged by the high levels of cortisol in my system.

In the early stages of pregnancy, I had reminded him that once the baby arrived, the baby would have to come first. He'd never be higher than number two on my list again. He looked slightly stunned, and a look washed over his face as if the penny had just dropped. Some blindly optimistic part of him had equated my maternity leave with me being there for *him* 24-7. He'd tried so hard to get me to give up work and be at home with him. He didn't understand that going to work was my sanity respite. Without work, I wouldn't have been able to cope with the life I led at home.

I was still in love with the carefree 31-year-old with the easy laugh. I hadn't seen that guy for a long time, but I never gave up hope that he was there, somewhere, inside the shell.

He is the one I grieved for.

I grieved for the broken boy failed by his parents.

I grieved for the young man trying to work through his recovery and be a better person.

I grieved for the man who was tender and loving to me.

I grieved for the man betrayed by those who claimed to love him.

And I grieved for the life we should have had, the life we might have had if only we'd been ready.

How We Began

We met just before Christmas 2004. I had left a corporate career that autumn to join a start-up. Within a couple of months, it became clear that I had made a huge mistake and, by December, I was job hunting.

One of the recruitment consultants I visited arranged a meeting with the general manager of the local newspaper for a chat, even though he didn't have any suitable vacancies at the time.

When I got to the newspaper offices, I was shown to a line of chairs in a passageway and told the manager would be with me soon. A friendly dog came to say hello and dropped white hair all over my black coat. I looked at the man behind the window in the far corner of the room beyond and hoped the chat wasn't going to be with him. Even from that distance, I could tell that the ability to speak might desert me if I was in a small room with him.

Sure enough, five minutes later, he strode towards me from his office, held out his hand with a grin and said, "Hello, I'm Oliver Lund." I shook his hand and said, "Hello, I'm Rhiannon" and then silently, "I'm going to marry you and have your babies."

It was the most instant connection I've ever had. Love at first sight, lust at first sight, who knows? But it was there from the first moment and it was real.

He showed me into his office and we had the weirdest possible version of a job interview. It notably featured the questions "Are you married?" – no – "Children?" – no. Reader, to this day, I wish I'd responded with "Why? Are you offering?" but I was stunned that he would just come out and ask such things!

We talked and laughed for more than two hours. His dog lay on my feet. I had face ache from grinning. We were only interrupted by his office manager who reminded him that some members of staff needed to see him before the Christmas party.

He gave me his card, told me he'd be in touch after the weekend to sort out another conversation with his boss, and then I was outside. Grinning and freezing, I knew everything had just changed.

When I didn't get a call on Monday morning, I phoned his office. "Oh, he's not in this week," came the response, and I was confused because I'd been so sure he would call me. Then the woman on the other end of the line told me he'd had a car accident on the way home from the party. He had, apparently, checked himself out of hospital that morning.

I called his mobile and he answered. We talked, I made him laugh. That wasn't so great for his bruised ribs, so I tried not to make him laugh. He sounded so happy to hear from me.

And that was how it began.

It could have been the opening of a great love story, but neither of us was ready to be in one of those.

He was still trying to extricate himself from a relationship that nobody in his life remembered fondly. I was still living in fear of an unstable ex and wasn't yet ready to fully trust anybody.

However, he became my Oliver and I became his Rhiannon. I sometimes referred to him as Ferrari Boy, and his staff at the newspaper apparently referred to me as Lara Croft. We spent several weekends together, walking on the beach and talking and eating and drinking gallons of tea, before we ever even kissed. He used to tease me and tell people I thought he was gay. I didn't. I just knew that he was every bit as scared as I was about this magnetic energy we felt between us.

Over time, we became lovers, and wove each other into the fabric of our respective lives. He regularly asked me to move in with him and have his babies; it took years before I agreed. We weren't a couple, though, not for a long time. I had seen too many of my friends curtail their lives to suit their partners, and I didn't want that.

His Family

His family dynamic was complicated. There is a tower on a hill in Yorkshire that legend says was built by his ancestors to celebrate one whole year without a family feud. Oliver described his own parents' divorce as being like the 1980s movie *War of the Roses*. Few opportunities for sniping and acrimony were ever passed up, even 25 years after that divorce.

Melissa, Oliver's younger sister, only properly met her father as an adult. As far as she could remember, he had been physically absent from every part of her childhood.

Erica, Oliver's stepmother, used to say, "If there was an easy way and a fucking awkward way to do anything, the Lunds would choose the latter."

She was a wise woman.

Oliver and his twin brother had been born prematurely. Research suggests that premature birth is closely linked to mental health issues later in life. When you add on the trauma they experienced in childhood, it is hardly surprising that neither of the twins flourished at school or followed traditional career paths.

Addiction

Oliver was severely dyslexic, and was told repeatedly that he was stupid and lazy. His self-esteem was not adequately nurtured during those formative years and he ended up with a strong sense of being 'less than' and not good enough.

By the time he was a teenager, he suffered from full blown self-loathing and was well on his way to being a chronic alcoholic. He was not the only one in his family with an unhealthy relationship with alcohol but, by the time I met him, he was sober and outwardly successful.

Sadly, it didn't last and, over the seven years I knew him, he had several relapses. By the time I issued my ultimatum, his alcoholism had such a tight grip on him that he didn't believe recovery was possible.

And if That's Not Complicated Enough

Then there was James. The boy I had loved and lost as a teenager. I felt responsible for his death.

Everything is amplified when you are young, because you have so little life experience from which to gain perspective. Things happen, and you take them to heart and they become part of who you are.

A wise lady called Daphne once told me that what we experience when we are young becomes part of our operating system. We may change or upgrade the things we use at application level, but if our operating system is not functioning correctly, we will never get the results we desire.

That conversation pre-dated smartphones and apps, and I had a limited grasp of how computers worked. But it made sense to me in its simplicity, that the hidden base level coding will impact the performance of everything else.

Your operating system level of processing is affected by how you grow up and the messages you absorb from the world around you. If you spend your childhood in complete security, knowing that you are loved and never having to worry about being cold or hungry, you will see the world differently from somebody who has grown up with the opposite.

You may recognise the following stories from among the people you know, or even in yourself.

The child who grows up in neglect and/or abuse is unlikely to develop strong self-esteem. Their perception of what is 'normal' will likely be warped by their experience.

The child of an acrimonious divorce who has grown up listening to the resident parent's bitterness and vitriol is likely to struggle to create healthy relationships later in life. Their operating system may have been imprinted with messages about how men/women cannot be trusted, or that everybody leaves you eventually, or that all that men/women care about is money and so on.

The child of a divorce that results in rarely seeing the non-resident parent is likely to grow up with a fear of abandonment.

The child who grows up as a carer may struggle to put themselves first as an adult.

The teenager who is already a bit fucked up is likely to take a throwaway comment to heart and believe that someone she loves has died because she said the wrong thing.

Unresolved feelings of guilt may then lead to shame.

Yes, that last one was me.

James

I met James when I was fifteen. He and his friends followed me and my friends down a busy city street, trying to get us to stop and talk to them. I threw some quips and walked faster, then realised my friends had stopped. I had to go back for them as I was the oldest and marginally more streetwise than they were.

The six of us ended up going to a bar and having a round of soft drinks in a slightly darkened booth. I remember James took my hand in his and looked at my palm. He showed me that we both had freckles in our palms and told me how rare that was. He looked deep into my eyes and, in combination with feeling sexual chemistry for the first time in my life, I was entranced.

I agreed to meet him again, just the two of us.

Optimistically, I hoped we were going on a date that would resemble what I had seen on television. In reality, we went to a skanky café for tea that was over-brewed and served in stained cups.

From there, we stopped by a market stall and he bought a bag of apples. Then we walked down to the water meadows. We walked and talked and walked. We talked about our hopes and dreams, history and darkness. He was older than me, maybe twenty, and seemed so wise.

He also told me about drugs, and warned me never to touch anything in powder or tablet form. He explained how dealers cut drugs with all sorts of things and how unscrupulous some of them are about what they add. That tip alone probably saved my life.

He was like a Billy Joel song. To begin with, he was *Uptown Girl*, as he went out of his way to show me that money got in the way of real connection. As time wore on, I began to think of him as *Innocent Man*.

I never saw him again after that day in the meadows. He went back to London and that was that.

But we spent hours on the phone in the year or two that followed. He would move house and call me to let me know the new number. He would call me at random times – sometimes during the day if he figured I might be at home because it was a weekend or school holiday, and sometimes in the evening.

He had a knack for calling me when I was feeling extremely low. He would listen, and then talk to me for as long as it took to get me level again or, better yet, laughing. He was my guardian angel.

One day, he called and said he wanted to come down to see me. He said he'd camp in the backyard if it made my parents happier. I freaked out and told him no. He tried to reassure me that it was all okay, but I ended up asking him not to call me again.

I'm not even sure where it came from. Maybe I'd been feeling dramatic or maybe I felt cornered, I don't remember.

In any case, he never called me again.

As I was about to sit my A-level exams, I bumped into one of the guys who'd been with him that first time we met. He said something about James frying his brain on acid and how he hardly knew who he was any more. I felt like this guy hated me, that he blamed me for the breakdown of his relationship with his friend.

After the exams, I went up to London. I wandered around

Blackheath trying to find the last address I had for James. I spoke to a stranger and asked if he knew the address I was struggling to find. He said it sounded like the annexe where someone had died a few weeks earlier.

I felt it must be him.

My teenage brain warped everything and I convinced myself that this was my fault. I had been so wrapped up in my own problems I hadn't realised that *he* needed *me*. I had pushed him away, even though all he had ever done was help me.

From there, it spiralled and I began to believe I was dangerous to the ones I loved. To protect them, I pushed away every boy who tried to shower me with the love I craved.

Even as I grew up and thought I'd put it all behind me, I continued to put the good guys firmly in the friend zone, where they were safe, instead of allowing my natural feelings to develop into something beautiful and life-enhancing.

In my early thirties, an old school friend told me she'd seen James. She was pretty sure he wasn't dead at all.

I'd spent seventeen years unable to let the Prince Charmings in my life near me, and it might all have been a tragic misunderstanding. Or worse, it might have been a prank.

His death was such a formative part of my story that being told it never happened shook me to my core. And then I realised that whether he'd died or not was now almost irrelevant. What was important was recognising the message that I had taken from that experience of feeling responsible for somebody else's life choices.

My Complicated Life

To get the greatest benefit from this book and the questions that it poses, I recommend that you use a notebook or journal and write down both the question and your answer.

1. What in this chapter did you relate to?

2. What in this chapter resonates with your 'origin story'?

3. What resonates with your relationships? Think about your family, friends, co-workers as well as your romantic partnerships here.

4. In what contexts or instances have you met your own expectations or those of others?

5. In what contexts have you gone against the grain and made choices that surprised others?

6. How did you feel when you made those choices?

Identity and the Widow Card

I was 34 when my Oliver died. He was 38 and our baby girl, Tilly, was 10 days old.

He wasn't my husband, but I am still his widow.

Sometimes you need to clarify that for people who like everything in tidy boxes, neatly wrapped up. Life isn't like that for me. I'm not sure it's that way for many people.

In fact, the government is quite happy for me to tick 'widowed' on my tax forms, but that's not enough for some people. It still irks me when I think of the old battleaxe at Erica's funeral who wanted me to explain why I sat at the front near the altar with the immediate family. When I said I was Oliver's widow she felt the need to say, "I didn't know he'd been married", as if a certificate was the only way to join a family. I sat at the front because my father-in-law asked me to sit there, with him, as a member of his close family.

A wedding is not what makes a family.

Sometimes a funeral is though.

Sometimes a funeral is as much a new beginning as it is a closure. People often say that as one chapter ends another begins. I knew it was true with regard to changing jobs or the ending of a relationship, but I had never thought about what that meant when it came to the end of someone's life.

I was now a widow, a member of a club I had never wanted to join and will never really leave.

A few years back, I read a very powerful blog by Michelle Steinke in which she talked about the 'widow police' wanting to revoke her membership of the widow club and have her membership card back because she had found love again. The concept of the widow card has stuck with me ever since. It is invisible, but we carry it.

For most people who aren't widows, the word has certain connotations.

I know it used to for me. First, you might think of an old lady, maybe with a blue rinse and sensible shoes. There's knitwear, short curly hair, a headscarf and jewellery. She might resemble a kind grandmother from a child's picture book. Or she might be a feisty and glamorous *Golden Girl*, or maybe a little more *Last of the Summer Wine*. If you find out that the widow is a younger woman, you might have this bizarre romanticised idea from the movies of some incredible love story cut short, maybe by a plane crash or cancer.

But what if that's not your story?

Other people's expectations of 'widow' status can be crippling, especially when you're just trying to work it out for yourself.

In my first couple of card-carrying years, I found that I spent an awful lot of time trying to help other people who felt they'd transgressed some unwritten law that you should never ask a widow about her status or her 'other half'. People are so shocked when you say, "Actually, he died" or "Actually, I'm a widow", that you can almost see them trying to crawl out of their own skin.

Some people are so uncomfortable with the idea that you might have an emotional reaction to something *they've* said that they scurry away as quickly as possible.

Others avoid speaking to you altogether once they know, just in case. Maybe they think it's contagious?

Then there are those who ask you a million questions about how your person died. Whatever label you or society assigns them – your husband, partner, loved one – they are, or were, your person. If you can't give those questioners a cut and dried car accident, or cancer, they keep digging. Sometimes you don't mind. But sometimes you really just want them to butt out and leave you alone.

Or maybe you have that feeling that the world's been avoiding you for days and you just need to talk to someone. So, you start to talk and you forget to breathe and a whole lot more comes out than was meant to. And then they're looking at you like you're losing it and you start to ask yourself why you're just talking and talking and talking…

Existing in a grief state can sometimes remove your filters, so you let things out that you probably shouldn't.

Like the time I took Tilly to a swimming lesson and the other mums were talking about getting together with their husbands and, even though none of them looked my way or asked me anything, I heard this voice telling them that mine was dead.

And that voice went on talking and we weren't in the changing room any more, we were in the lesson and the voice kept talking about him and about how much pain he'd been in and the teacher kept trying to change the channel, but the voice, my voice, carried on.

I'd forgotten about that day until I bumped into the swimming instructor a year or so later. By then, I was in a different space. We were joking about something and she started to tell me about how you wouldn't believe what some people talked about in the lessons. And then she realised that one of those people had been me.

Remembering brought up feelings of shame. I felt ashamed that I had transgressed. I had shared my darkness in the wrong place and, in doing so, had upset some people.

But, at the time, I was just trying to keep breathing, keep my head above water, by releasing a chunk of concrete from my body so that I could float.

I was carrying too many burdens, and other people's expectations were not top of my list.

According to fork theory, I was pulling a fork out of my flesh. I heartily recommend you read more about fork theory if this concept makes sense to you (jenrose.com/fork-theory/). Essentially, fork theory is about the amount of weight/pressure/stress/irritation you can handle.

Your personal limit could be reached by four big things, or a million little things – like the straw that broke the camel's back. When you feel you're getting close to your limit, you can relieve the pressure by "pulling out a fork", even if it seems smaller or unrelated.

The brilliant example given on the web address I flagged above is going to the toilet in the middle of a conversation, because pulling out the little fork of needing to pee makes space to receive the bigger fork of something like a financial burden.

The expectations of people outside the circle of grief don't really matter in the grand scheme of things, but it can be hard to gain perspective when you're living in the shadow. If you feel that people, albeit in a caring and well-meaning way, are watching you, it's even worse. I felt torn between putting on an "I'm fine. You can leave me alone now" show all the time and feeling that I should be more visibly devastated by everything all the time.

The thing is, there is no *should* here.

We carry this huge weight of the burden of others' expectations and we don't need to.

Is that easier said than done? Of course.

It is worth considering that we are also carrying the weight of what we *think* other people's expectations of us are. Read that again.

When the foundations of our identity start to shift, we lose confidence – if we had it to begin with – in our value as people in our own right. What this means is that when we are not feeling strong in our own identity, we start to worry more about what other people think of us. Unfortunately, our brains are wired to think that other people are thinking negatively. As Julia Roberts said in *Pretty Woman*, "The bad stuff is easier to believe."

So, we may actually be making life a lot more difficult for ourselves simply by listening to the chatter in our own heads. Have you ever asked someone how *they* think you *should* be behaving or coping or expressing yourself?

Yes, some people will have opinions and some people will be judgy.

The thing is, the people who matter will not judge you. They will not run from you and they will not stop loving you. The people who can't cope with you at your worst may not be the right people to still be there when you're at your best.

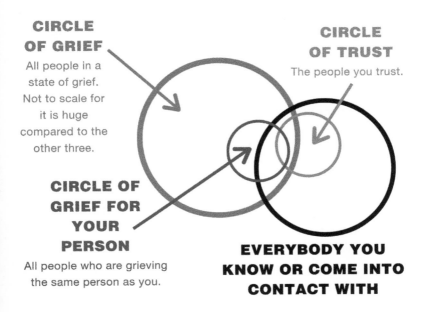

CIRCLE OF GRIEF
All people in a state of grief. Not to scale for it is huge compared to the other three.

CIRCLE OF TRUST
The people you trust.

CIRCLE OF GRIEF FOR YOUR PERSON
All people who are grieving the same person as you.

EVERYBODY YOU KNOW OR COME INTO CONTACT WITH

Then there are the people inside the circle. The circle of grief isn't the same as the circle of trust. The people inside the circle of grief are also grieving. There's a wider circle of grief containing people in a grief state for other people, and a smaller circle for the people who are also grieving your person.

In this smaller circle, the pressure can be suffocating, or explosive.

In the latter years of his life, Oliver had struggled a great deal with most things. His personal relationships had all suffered and, while his funeral was very well attended, there weren't that many people who were *really* in his life.

In his death, when he could no longer speak for his side of the story, there were some who suddenly claimed to having been incredibly close with him.

They may have been. But, then again, they may not.

I trawled through the years that Oliver and I had known each other, through the thousands of hours on the phone and the months we had lived together, listening while he told me about each and every thing he'd done and who he'd spoken to. But I couldn't place the closeness that some other grieving individuals described to me. It didn't ring true.

The best I could do was distance myself to avoid having to listen to it, so that it wouldn't irritate me as much. Because it did irritate me, a lot.

It pressed my buttons. If you were so close, why did you never visit him?

If you were so close, why did all of your phone conversations sound like you wanted to set each other on fire with the sheer force of your mutual loathing?

If you were so close, why did you say such vile things to me about him behind his back?

If you were so close, why did he warn me never to trust you?

If you were so close, why did you never show up when he needed you?

If you were so close, why were you so relentlessly selfish?

Because if you really were so close, you must have known how much pain he was in and how desperate he was feeling?

My desire to lash out and verbalise how insane it all sounded made me twitch.

But my inner voice kept reminding me that we all grieve in our own way, and everybody was dealing with the guilt they felt in their own way too. It felt as if certain people were resolutely pushing that guilt away from themselves and onto others. They did not fill the Oliver circle. There were also those who internalised their grief and took that guilt upon and into themselves. From my perspective, they were not the people who had guilt to claim.

The burden of expectations weighs heavy. Some expectations are external, but many come from within ourselves. I felt an expectation to form relationships with members of Oliver's family, because of our daughter. I felt an expectation to try to integrate all of these extra people into our lives because they were links to her father and bits of his life that I hadn't been part of. Maybe, in hindsight, those people felt that expectation too, because most hadn't seen Oliver at all during his final couple of years when I had been there for so much of it. Oliver was unpredictable and his behaviour could be erratic. As he declined, he pushed away the people he loved.

When I kissed his corpse in the funeral home, it was the first time I had been in the same room with him for three months.

It didn't hurt any less, just because we'd already been apart for a while.

It didn't hurt any less, just because we hadn't spoken.

It didn't hurt any less. It hurt more.

He was dressed in the Guernsey jumper my parents had bought him for Christmas and a pair of jeans. His perfect lips were set in a little half smile, he was finally at peace. He had no shoes on and I worried that his feet might be cold. Of course they were cold, he was dead.

Rationality goes out of the window though, doesn't it?

It all feels surreal and like a weird dream.

You start the day making love, end it in an argument and then the next thing you know you're kissing a corpse.

I went from being me, pregnant and a bit sad that his drinking was spiralling out of control, to being a widow with a ten-day old baby and no idea who I was any more, in what felt like a single day.

I had moved back in with my parents. The dining room surfaces were covered with cards – some congratulating me on the birth of my baby and others offering me deepest sympathy. It was an overwhelming emotional rollercoaster.

There I was, full of hormones from bringing a new life into the world and, at the same time, being crushed by the devastation of grief.

When I wasn't in the darkness, my body and soul wracked with pain, I was numb. I was exhausted from the combination of having a new born and being on this emotional rollercoaster. I couldn't figure out whether I should be cooing at my baby or throwing myself under a train. I didn't know which way was up. If my parents hadn't been so hands-on, actively keeping us both alive, I don't know if we'd have made it.

It's hard to say that out loud, but there's not much point writing a book about the truth setting you free if you don't walk the walk. So, there it is. I don't know if we'd have made it.

Breathe.

Luckily for us, I have incredible parents who have walked alongside me, held my hand, helped me up and, at times, shoved me up the hill of life. I can see how far I've come and I am relieved and proud of my efforts, but mostly I'm grateful to all of the people who have helped keep my trajectory one of growth.

In that initial phase of grief, though, growth was so far from my mind, as if it didn't exist. Survival was about as far as I could get.

Layers of Identity

I have spoken to a lot of other mums over the past few years about that loss of identity we feel when we become secondary to our offspring. The moment they leave our bodies and take their first breath, they usurp us.

No matter who you were before you had a baby – surgeon, CEO, PA, stripper – as soon as that little person emerges, you become a mum – food source, bum wiper, bag carrier, taxi driver, nurse, photographer and so many other things besides. You get lost for a bit. You become your baby's everything, and no longer a person in your own right.

At baby groups, you sit with women you might never otherwise have met, discussing sleep deprivation and mastitis. The fruit of your womb is what bonds you to these women. The playing fields are levelled by joining this motherhood club. This common ground you share is enough. Or is it?

I sometimes wonder how adoptive mums feel when surrounded by women swapping birth stories and complaining of sore nipples. I guess they feel slightly apart.

I felt slightly apart.

There were whole conversations revolving around husbands, fiancés and boyfriends. I couldn't join in with those. I couldn't even connect with the mum who had gone down the donor route. I don't even remember her name. I still have contacts in my phone where the mother's name is followed by the name of her offspring.

The portal to motherhood is a one-way ticket. There is no going back. Once through, you are your child's mother until you die. It is a layer of identity that is permanently bonded to you, and changes both how you see the world and how the world sees you.

Widowhood operates in the same way. Once you are a widow, you are a widow for the rest of your life. It changes how you see the world, and when the world knows you have that layer, it changes how it sees you.

When you have both motherhood and widowhood, you have two layers of identity placed on top of your own.

It felt a bit like being buried alive.

People no longer met me as *me* first.

For me, this was exacerbated by moving to the countryside, where my parents lived, hours away from my friends. I was heavily pregnant, knew nobody, and I was feeling pretty flattened because Oliver had chosen alcohol over us. I filled my time preparing for the baby and hiding from the reality of my life. I sewed and knitted and drank tea and went to midwife appointments. I had limited opportunities to make new friends – more on that later – which meant that by the time I was meeting people, I was both a mother and a widow.

Most of them met me first as Tilly's mum, some of them then met me as Oliver's widow. Many have stuck around to get to know *me*, but it took time.

Your identity may feel squashed, or even lost. It may be screaming to get to the surface, or it may be quite happy to hide for a bit. The important thing is to never lose sight of the fact that it exists. You can reinvent yourself if you need to, because you are more than the carrier of bags and expectations.

I still don't know if I want my identity to be forever *about* being a widow, but I know it will always be a part of me. Accepting and embracing that part of me has been key to my growth and my ability to move forwards.

Who am I?

When you feel ready to explore what lies beneath the layers of 'widow' and/or 'parent', here are a few questions for you to think about. To get the most benefit, get out your journal and write out the questions along with your answers. And, please, be honest with yourself.

1. What are the layers of my identity right now?

   a. How do other people see me?

      This is about *your* perceptions of how they see you, but if you want to ask other people how they see you, you might be pleasantly surprised with what they say. It might be helpful to split people into two categories:

      i. People who know me well

      ii. People who know me less well

   b. How do I see myself?

      You might find it helpful to look in the mirror and look yourself in the eyes, or to look through photos from years ago, months ago and now.

   c. How do I feel about those layers?

      There are no right or wrong answers, but you might find it useful to be able to come back to these answers later, to see a change.

2. What roles do I play in my life?

   This is about your active participation and where you use your time and energy. This may include work, parenting, wider family responsibilities, volunteering, and so on.

3. Am I happy with my identity and the way I am living my life right now?

4. If I am not happy with my identity, what would I like to feel differently about?

Suicide is Painless

I remember singing the MASH theme song at school when I was ten or eleven years old in music class with Mr Ridgeway. I look back now and wonder why on earth he chose that song for us, with its macabre title and themes. Maybe he knew that among us would be a handful whose lives had been or would be touched by suicide. Or maybe he just liked the song.

The lyrics are beautifully simple. That's because they were written by a fourteen-year-old boy. Robert Altman, who directed MASH, wanted it to be "the stupidest song ever written" and passed the task over to his son when he couldn't write it himself. Amusingly, Altman made less than $100,000 for directing the movie but his son made over $1 million for co-writing the song.

If Mr Ridgeway had chosen it with foresight, I wonder if he

knew how many times suicide would touch my life.

I don't know what the UK suicide rate was back in the 1980s but, at a conference I attended towards the end of 2019, I discovered that, in Cornwall, there is one death by suicide every five days. Three out of four of those deaths are men.

Until I did some research, I was unaware that hanging is the most popular method for those planning to die by suicide. It shouldn't have come as a surprise, given that, of the three people I personally know who have definitely died by suicide, two went with hanging.

And two of those three fit the stats of being men under the age of 45.

One was a classmate at night school when I was 19. I wish I could remember his name. We were a motley crew ranging from me, aged 19, to a woman in her 60s. We were all a bit shy during the first few lessons, but gradually started contributing to discussions. He was a nice, gentle guy, probably in his 30s. He rode a motorbike and was the object of quiet crushes from several corners of the room. He never gave any indication to any of us that he was in pain, or down. One week he simply didn't show up, and the next week our tutor gave us the news that he had hanged himself. We were all stunned.

A year or two later, during fresher's week in my hall of residence, I spent some time with Miles. He was funny and full of vigour, wildly attractive, with a glint of dangerous unpredictability in his eye. We had some fun and might have ended up good friends if circumstances hadn't caused our paths to diverge. Years later, I found out that he too had died by suicide.

Erica

Then, in March 2018, so much closer to home, I received the news that my beloved Erica, Oliver's stepmother and Tilly's darling Grannie, had hanged herself.

It was a Sunday morning and there was a missed call from her number on my mobile. This was a little unusual as, although we texted and talked on the phone, I was always the one to initiate contact.

I called her back and somebody answered who was not Erica. She thought I was somebody else, and when I said, "No, it's Rhiannon. Who is this?" she told me I must call Colin and Melissa.

I knew that whatever it was, it must be awful, and I shut myself in the bathroom with shaking hands. Tilly was playing in her bedroom next door, and I didn't want her to hear.

Colin and Melissa were in shock too, and delivered the news quite bluntly. She was dead. She had hanged herself.

My beloved Erica. She had been a great friend to me and she was a natural Grannie. Her entire adult life revolved around looking after other people – her mother, her mother-in-law, her husband. And it wore her out.

In the final months of her life, we had spoken about carer fatigue and she couldn't see a way that her lot in life would ever improve. She had been hospitalised several times with exhaustion. She would rest and recover and be discharged with antidepressants instead of support.

John, my father-in-law, had some pretty archaic ideas about gender roles in their marriage. He loved Erica and spoke very highly of her to anyone who would listen. When he showed me their wedding photographs, I asked him how on earth he'd snared such a beauty. He knew how lucky he was to have her.

As he got older and his health declined, he seemed to expect to be waited on, and for Erica to do it all with a smile. Even before he broke his hip and was confined to a wheelchair, I don't believe I ever saw him make a cup of tea.

From what Erica told me, and what others witnessed, John had quickly become comfortable sitting in his wheelchair asking people to get and do things for him, rather than doing the physical therapy that would get him walking again. He became even more demanding.

Some of this was doubtless due to his regular urinary tract infections, which had a heavy impact on his moods and behaviour. But knowing he was in the grip of an infection didn't make coping with being on the receiving end any easier.

He would agree that she needed to rest more, but his behaviour never offered her the opportunity. They had external carers who came in when Erica couldn't physically manage, but there was little respite. I often wonder if it might have turned out differently if he'd been open to the idea of going into a nursing home. Sadly, that wasn't how things panned out, and she hanged herself.

The entire time I knew Erica, she talked about needing to use Valium and diazepam. I was never quite sure if she was joking or not. Physically, she was as delicate as a bird and had obviously been struggling emotionally for some time. The last time she was released from hospital, we had expected a care plan to be quickly put in place. We imagined more external carer input, and that it would happen quickly. Instead, she was given more antidepressants.

Reaching the point where death by suicide feels like the only option can sometimes happen quickly and sometimes slowly. Sometimes it feels that way for a long time before the person takes action. Sometimes the pain for the sufferer is so acute that, to the rest of us left behind, the final action feels as if it has come from nowhere.

Did I feel guilty for Erica?

Of course, I did. I should have called more often. I should have made myself call every week. I should not have believed her when she said she was okay. I should have run up a credit card bill in plane tickets, to get to her and help her out. I should have been willing to do all of those things, but I wasn't. I was barely holding it together in my own life.

I could have texted her more. I could have sent her a text every night to remind her that she was loved from afar and I could have sent her a text every morning to help her gird herself for another day. But I didn't.

I didn't know what to say to help her get through because, honestly, I couldn't see a way out for her either.

Society's expectations make it excruciatingly difficult for someone to throw their hands in the air and scream, "I don't want to do this any more," when they are married to somebody who needs to be looked after. You may feel that you cannot simply walk away. You may feel that you cannot initiate divorce proceedings to sever ties. You may feel that you cannot live with yourself for wanting the other person to die first so that you can have a chance to someday breathe the sweet air of freedom. You may feel trapped by the expectations of others just as surely as if you were manacled.

I know other women in very similar situations to Erica's, who have been caring, largely unsupported, for demanding, unappreciative and sometimes abusive husbands. They do not feel they would be 'allowed' to divorce those men and try to move on with their lives. So, they wait for their husbands to die. Feeling obliged to care for somebody for the rest of your life, who you no longer love or like, must be a very tough burden to shoulder.

I wasn't surprised that Erica had taken matters into her own hands. She had said things in the previous six months that meant I wasn't blindsided by that part. The part that shocked me was her chosen method. She didn't go with an overdose of pills for a gentle transition from this world to the next. She hanged herself. Yes, I've said that multiple times, because it still haunts me.

I wish it could have been different. But I know that wishing doesn't change anything.

I had to tell Tilly that morning that her Grannie was now with Daddie. I had to hold her as we both sobbed. I had to do the truth, but not the whole truth, all over again. I reminded her how Grannie had been in hospital a few times because her heart was so frail. I said she had worn herself out and now she was at peace, with her dogs Spinner and Weaver and her own Mummy.

The truth, but not the whole truth. Not yet.

Initially, I told the same story to my friends. *She was worn out and now she was gone.* A week or two later, I told them the rest because I needed to be able to lean on them and it felt unfair not to let them know why I was taking it so hard.

It also felt unfair not to explain to them more fully because I had voiced my mistrust in antidepressants again. Among this group of friends is at least one person who has been taking antidepressants for years, and who had reacted defensively when my feelings about them came up in conversation before. It was never my intention to make them feel attacked by my comments.

I had lashed out because I was frightened that our magic pill society would rob me of other people I loved.

So many people seem to be given a prescription for pills instead of the support they actually need.

Back to Oliver...

How about Oliver? Did he kill himself?

My mother assured me that nobody would ask how Oliver died. She was optimistic and sadly mistaken. I was asked by several people, some with the very open, "How did he die?" and a couple with an almost flippant, "Did he kill himself?"

It took me a long time to find peace with what had happened to him in the years running up to his premature death. Before that process was complete, I struggled with how to answer those questions. I wished so badly that he could have been killed in a car accident, so that I had a straightforward explanation and nobody would ask for more details.

I am still friends with most of the people who asked how he died. I'm sure they were trying to help me to open up and unburden myself but, at the time, it felt like morbid curiosity and an intrusion. In some ways, moving to a different area within months of Oliver's death, where nobody knew us, was a blessing. It gave me the opportunity to tell his story in my own time. But in other ways, it made it more difficult because I had to keep telling his story to a fresh audience.

I see suicide as an active word. I'm glad we no longer say 'commit suicide' the way we used to. It sounded like a crime, too akin to 'commit murder'. Following a campaign by the Samaritans, we now have 'death by suicide', i.e., he died by suicide or she died by suicide or they died by suicide.

It's a death, not a murder.

Did Oliver die by suicide?

In my way of understanding what happened that night, no.

I think there is a more passive way to die that is, as yet, unnamed. Maybe death by spiritual exhaustion? When a person no longer has the will to fight for their life, but lacks the drive to end it. I think this better describes where Oliver ended up.

He had chronic nerve pain following a number of injuries and the pain was constant.

The ankle pain went back to his youth. He'd broken both ankles – one from crashing a motorised skateboard – and had metalwork in his body as a result. Neither ankle ever looked quite right.

In his mid-thirties, he was hit by a car. I don't remember the details, but I think it may have been on a dual carriageway. He'd got out of the car during an argument with the mother of his firstborn child and was hit by another vehicle.

A few months later, in an incident with the police, he cut his right arm. In the absence of a number of freak circumstances that night, he probably wouldn't have survived. His life was saved and his arm was reconstructed, but he was never the same again.

The painkillers prescribed by medical professionals took the edge off the day-to-day pain but couldn't touch his acute flare ups. Sometimes he could manage as much as a week without having one but, at other times, they came daily.

Had he been happy to take the pills and do nothing all day but take gentle strolls, watch TV and do his physio, maybe he would have avoided those acute episodes. But, for a man in his 30s, that is simply not living.

He loved driving, as long as it was fast. Especially if it was fast and had racetrack curves to throw the car into. The vibration of the steering wheel would trigger spasms and flare ups. I lost count the number of times he stopped at traffic lights and said, "You need to drive now", and we'd run around the car to swap seats before the lights changed.

He loved sailing, but could no longer hold the ropes.

He loved me, but couldn't do any of the lifting and carrying to help me when we moved house. Given that I was seven months pregnant, I couldn't do it either and I had to call my father. It bothered Oliver immensely that my father had to step in to fulfil a role that he could not. He worried endlessly over whether he'd be able to manage holding the baby when she came.

His identity as a man was threatened by the frailty of his body.

The scope of his life had become incredibly limited.

He wasn't a great patient. He was probably a nightmare for his medical team. He drank tea and coffee all day, chewed coffee beans in the evening and took sleeping tablets at night. He met the suggestion that he switch to decaf with contempt.

His acute flare ups were often triggered by his attempts to live beyond the parameters of his broken body, and he would take more pills in an attempt to bring himself down from the ceiling. I saw him, too many times to count, in the foetal position, his entire body clenched in agony.

If somebody had told him in those moments that drinking drain cleaner would take the pain away, he probably would have considered it.

I wasn't with him the night he died. I read the paperwork, I listened to the coroner and I listened to the people he'd spoken to that day. He died on his sofa, in front of the TV.

His last day alive was 31 October 2011. It had not been a good day. The ongoing vitriolic dispute with his neighbour had escalated again, and the friend who had been with him that day had had enough of listening to the arguments. She went home and took her phone off the hook.

Oliver took his pills. From what the coroner said, he hadn't actually taken that many, given how many I knew he'd often take in order to get a decent night's sleep. At some point in the small hours, maybe he realised that this time he wouldn't wake up. He left a message on the answerphone of the friend who had been with him earlier in the day. He didn't call an ambulance. He went to sleep. Maybe he didn't care if he woke up, or maybe he was just too drowsy to make a 999 call.

By the time she had got out of bed and checked her phone, he was gone.

In my eyes, that wasn't an active suicide; it was a death by not having enough fight left to survive.

The coroner gave a narrative verdict and kindly told me that it was probably the most peaceful way a person can slip from one world to the next. That gave me great comfort.

I was glad for Oliver that his pain was over. He no longer had to deal with the constant attacks on his nervous system and pain receptors.

He no longer had to worry about his neighbour attacking him in his sleep or poisoning his dog.

He no longer had to worry about the police turning up and treating him like a hardened criminal.

He no longer had to worry about whether I would ever forgive him and let him back in.

He no longer had to worry about anything.

He was finally at peace.

For the rest of us, it was anything but peaceful.

Whenever somebody dies, even when it's expected, there are

things left unfinished. There are things we said or did that we wish we hadn't, and there are things we wish that we had said or done but that we never got around to. Those loose ends dangle in our minds and, if we let them, they can strangle us.

By the time he died, Oliver had alienated most of the people who loved him. He had so successfully pushed away the people he loved that none of us were there to catch him when he fell. Over a year earlier, he had told me that this was something he was doing deliberately, because he thought it would make his death less painful for those, he suspected, he would leave behind.

By the time he asked me back into his life early in 2010, he was sure that he didn't have long left. The bleeding and abdominal pain he suffered convinced him he had cancer. The cause was most likely ulcers – he was highly strung and on a pharmaceutical cocktail that would rot anybody's guts. His body felt as if it was falling apart and nobody in his medical teams had instilled any sense of hope that his situation could be resolved.

I cannot imagine that pain management is a field that any medic enters lightly, with few happy outcomes. I watched the Paralympics the year after Oliver died, and the Invictus Games two years after that. I listened to awe-inspiring competitors who talked about the pain they lived with every day, some mentioning the fentanyl patches (an opioid pain medication) that Oliver had been unable to function without. I watched, I listened and I cried.

Why couldn't he have been more like them?

Why couldn't he have found a mind over matter response to the pain?

Why couldn't he still be here, sitting on the sofa beside me, watching his ridiculously enormous bloody TV?

From what I have seen and read, mind over matter is the key to living with chronic pain. If a person has mental strength, they can access a resilience way beyond the physical. Oliver had been fighting for his life since his premature arrival in Swindon in 1973, and

I think he'd used up every ounce of strength he had, and then some, by the time he left us.

Suicide is rarely painless.

For Oliver, I believe his death was the most painless bit of his later life, whether it was intentional or not. Nobody else was there, so nobody can say for sure.

He wasn't drunk when he died. For an alcoholic who struggled so hard with his demons, that is an important thing to mention.

Why did I write about suicide in this book if I don't believe Oliver died that way? This is a question someone asked after reading an early draft of the book. The thing is, I *have* been affected by suicide, and Erica came into my life through Oliver's death. And if any of my story helps somebody move forward from losing a loved one to suicide, it's worth it.

Shame

When you are left behind after a person you love dies because of an accidental overdose, or an active suicide, or some other messy death, you may feel compelled to take on a burden of shame.

Brene Brown argues that guilt is associated with behaviour, but shame is associated with identity. It is the difference between 'I did something bad' and 'I am bad'.

You may not have done anything wrong or foolish. You may not have had anything to do with that person's decision to die, or to give up the fight. You may feel shame because of societal pressures around death and what is and is not deemed an acceptable way to go.

In the recent past, dying from AIDS was seen as such a shameful thing that families abandoned their offspring to die alone. Being gay and having an active sex life was treated as a deplorable life choice. Much of our society has moved on from that viewpoint. We now live in a more inclusive society that sees the outdated treatment of people who love differently as shameful.

But, in some communities, death by suicide still carries shame by association.

It shouldn't, because that association stops people getting help before they choose to die and it stops people getting help when they are the ones left behind.

It's a death, not a murder.

Suicide is not painless.

Suicide and Me

These questions will not be for everyone.

If this chapter has read like part of a story but not resonated with you, please just move on to the next chapter.

If you have been affected by suicide and want to go through the prompts, please remember to be gentle with yourself. Ideally, go through them when somebody else is around to comfort you if it brings up too much.

When you feel ready to, get out your journal. Write down each question, followed by your response.

1. What feelings did this chapter bring up for me?

2. Who have I known through my life who has died by suicide?

3. Look at each person individually on your list and ask yourself:

   a. Do I blame myself?

      i. Why?

      ii. What do I feel guilty for?

      iii. Does this guilt help anyone?

   b. Do I blame anyone else?

      i.   Why?

     ii.   Does this blame help anyone?

   iii. What does blaming them do to me?

  c. Do I feel affected by their death?

  d. Would I feel differently about their death if I didn't feel guilty?

The purpose of this exercise is not to encourage you to beat yourself up, but to help you to release the guilt and anger that can build up inside all of us. If we don't find ways to let go of it, it can eat away at us and be very detrimental to our mental health.

If you are seeking help from a counsellor or bereavement specialist, they may be happy to go through these prompts with you.

Part Two

Survival

PART TWO

A year today
Since you slipped away,
Three hundred and sixty-six days -
Some full of tears and laughter, others just a haze.
I feel you watching over us
Sat beside me in the car
Haunting me through the radio
Letting me know you've not gone far.
Your legacy is safe with me
Your secrets I will keep
Happy memories dancing in my mind
Whilst peacefully you sleep.
A missing piece that will not mend,
You were my lover and my friend.

1.11.12

Sequences and Deadlines

How long will I feel like this?

How long will it hurt like this?

When will I be myself again?

Will I *ever* be myself again?

When will I be able to laugh without feeling guilty that I am laughing and he is dead?

When will people stop looking at me with that desperately uncomfortable expression?

When will I not want to hit people who talk to me about moving on?

When will I be ready to tell our kid about him as he actually was?

These are questions I asked, and they are variations on the

questions I have been asked by friends who are at earlier stages in their journey through grief.

We live in an age of information overload, so we are drawn to simplistic explanations of things because it saves time and brain strain. When we are trying to function in a thick fog of grief, our need for simple explanations is all the stronger.

There's this simple view that grief has clearly recognised stages. It makes it sound like a flow chart where you go in at one end and pass through the stages and come out the other end and you're fine.

There are probably other versions, but the one I have heard most often goes like this: 1. Denial and Isolation; 2. Anger; 3. Bargaining; 4. Depression; 5. Acceptance. The fact that they are numbered makes it sound like there's a sequence. And, if there's a sequence, then surely when you've found acceptance around this person being dead and around the void they have left, then you're fine. You've come to the end of grief.

But no. You're not bloody fine.

I don't recognise the flow chart from my experience, and nor do any of my friends who have been through grief. It is too simplistic. You go through these stages over and over again. Sometimes it feels like you're stuck in a pinball machine that keeps catapulting you back to random feelings with no sequence at all.

There are some things that seem to happen in sequence, but you cannot rely upon one thing following the other where grief is concerned. It can feel like you're in one of those movies where the floor moves, or in *Indiana Jones and The Last Crusade* where you have to work out exactly where to step next, and it's not as straightforward as one foot in front of the other.

Grief is not linear and it is unfair to give people the impression that it is.

When I think about my early losses, where my relationship with that soul was simple and unconditional, maybe. Maybe that was a linear process.

Pip

I'm thinking about Pip. He came into my life when I was four years old and left when I was sixteen. In my eyes, he could do no wrong. To me, his breath never stank, although everyone else assured me that it really, really did. To me, his occasional episodes of geriatric deep sleep incontinence were nothing to worry about. To me, he was perfect. I loved him and he loved me and neither one of us ever questioned that. He never let me down, and he never showed it when I let him down. The day I came home from school and he didn't rush to the door to greet me, I knew it was time. It was his way of telling me he had had enough. It was a Friday and we spent the weekend together and he ate his favourite foods and we cuddled a lot. After school on Monday, we took him to the vet and I held him as his body slipped into the endless dreamy sleep and his soul scampered joyfully across the rainbow bridge.

Like many children, my first real experience of death and grief was for my beloved dog.

I felt responsible for his death, because it was my call, but I also knew I had done the right thing by him. The only guilt I felt was for not spending more time with him. I cried for two days and then I went back to school and the friends who had been through this themselves welcomed me into a knowing embrace. I still have a photo album of mostly terrible photos I took of my dog during my childhood, and a little envelope full of his hair. More than twenty-five years later, I still have the watercolour I painted of him hanging by my bed.

Looking back, the stages of grief were complicated then too. I don't remember feeling anger. For a long time before that day, I was definitely in denial that he was getting old, but I went from there to sad and then to acceptance in a matter of days. He'd been an endlessly happy dog, and I knew he wouldn't have wanted me to be sad. Acceptance didn't mean it didn't hurt any more, or that I stopped crying. No matter who you grieve for, acceptance simply means that you are accepting the new reality that you are now living and your friend or love is not and never will be again.

The loss of a furry companion should never be underestimated. For those of us who love our pets like family, their passing is a source of very deep and real pain. When Gemma died a year or so after Pip, we had to come home to an empty house at the end of each day and it was horrible. When you have known rapturous welcome for the best part of twenty years and then come home to nothing, the silence and emptiness are vast. I was grateful to go travelling and not to have to come home for a few months.

The air of sadness in the house did not dissipate, however. No sooner had I set off on my adventure than my mother's life was turned upside down by her father's cancer diagnosis. He died seven months later, just before I turned nineteen.

Grandpa

Grandpa's death wasn't so straightforward for me. My teenage years had not been light and fluffy, and I'd been resentful in his presence for a lot longer than that. In the mid-1980s, when we moved to the UK from Australia, where I had spent the first ten years of my life, my grandparents took us in.

My parents had bought a house near our school, but it wasn't ready to move into yet. My brother, who was 12 at the time, and ten-year-old me boarded at school and had these weird and exhausting fractured weekends with our parents. We had classes on Saturday mornings, and would then be collected by our parents and taken for lunch before the 60-mile drive back up to London to where my grandparents lived.

Twenty-four hours later, we would be back in the car again and on our way back to school. My grandparents put us up for months, accommodating a young and growing family in the way that only wonderful and loving parents and grandparents can.

I can see that now. But as a tired ten-year-old who never had any time to herself, I just wanted to be left alone. I didn't want to have to repeat everything about my week that I'd already said over lunch for this new audience. I didn't want to have to make polite small talk. I wanted to go hide in my room with Pip and read a book. I wanted to occasionally have my parents to myself, and that simply wasn't possible with six of us in the house. I was tired. I hated the toing and froing of weekly boarding.

My frustrations with our circumstances coloured my relationship with my grandparents.

Grandpa tried so hard to reconnect with me. In hindsight, I can see it as clear as day. He made dad jokes that irritated rather than softened me. One Christmas, I said some truly awful things about elderly drivers and he nearly looked angry, but mostly disappointed. It's hard to look back and not feel ashamed of how incredibly ungrateful and self-centred I was.

In January 1996, the entire family, including all three of my grandparent's children and all eight of their grandchildren, were together for their golden wedding anniversary. This was close to a once in a lifetime occasion. My mother's eldest brother was in the Australian military, and he and his family happened to be in the UK on a one-year posting.

A day or two after the anniversary celebrations, I went travelling and we were never all together in the same room again. My parents and I had made an agreement that, if there was nothing I could do, even by coming back, they simply wouldn't tell me any bad news until I got home. We all knew it would be the only time in my life when I would have no responsibilities beyond myself. However, we had no way of knowing how quickly my grandfather would go downhill.

He had been suffering with shoulder pains for years, but would brush off any fuss. My mother took him to see her chiropractor, and the x-rays showed huge holes in his shoulder blades. He was riddled with bone cancer. He had probably been in agony for years. He never complained. I think that surviving a prisoner of war camp and the Long March gave him such an extreme perspective of what pain, hardship and suffering were, that he refused to moan.

The first I knew that something was awry was when I visited my other grandpa in Canberra and he asked about the test results. "Tests?" I asked and Pa's face went pale, then he tried to backpedal. But he knew he'd screwed up. Bless him, his Alzheimer's was taking hold and he was at an age where everyone he knew was waiting on test results for something.

A phone call to my father that night joined dots I hadn't noticed up to now. Recently, my mother was never home when I called. But my calls were always sporadic and without warning, back in the days of phonecards and reverse charges. We didn't have texting or WhatsApp, Facebook or other social media to stay connected. We didn't even have email. When I went away, I essentially stepped off the edge of the world. I didn't have a weekly call slot, I was hopeless at letters and, when I was having fun, I would lose weeks before thinking to phone home.

My dad reminded me of our agreement. He promised he wouldn't say a word and nobody need ever know that we had spoken. I could choose to carry on with my plan and nobody would think any less of me, because as far as they were all aware, I had no idea about what was happening at home. A month earlier, Grandpa had been given two weeks to live. Dad assured me there was very little chance I would make it home in time, even if I managed to get on a flight for the first leg back the next day.

Nobody would think any less of me. Except me. I would definitely have thought *a lot* less of me.

I confided in the family friends I was staying with in Sydney and went straight to the STA office the next morning to see by how much we could shorten my trip.

In deciding to return home, I lost hundreds of dollars in nonrefundable trips I'd already booked in New Zealand. My four-week stay in that country became twenty minutes running across an airport terminal. I couldn't get in and out of Fiji without staying for a week because the flights were full. My planned road trip up the west coast of America and through Canada became a hugely expensive series of flights to New York, where I was ripped off and frightened by an unscrupulous taxi driver.

I had been dreaming of and planning this trip for years, but from the moment Pa said the word 'tests', it all went to shit.

I spoke to my father again to confirm that he could drive to Heathrow to pick me up, and that I wasn't too late. I assured him that, even if I missed saying goodbye to my grandpa, I knew my mother would need me. As it turned out, I had originally been due back to the UK on 12 July. I cut everything short and landed on 4 May. Grandpa died on 13 July. It seemed as if he'd fixed in his mind that he would stay with us until I was safely back and, even though he saw me, his countdown remained fixed.

On a visit to the hospice, I gave him his last laugh. I couldn't bear to see him in that state. This once great man, with the strength of twelve oxen, who could fix anything and would help anybody, was now skeletal and yellow and barely moving. I struggled to find words to speak to him, so I did my take on the Rimmer triple-double salute from *Red Dwarf* and it made him smile and painfully chuckle. I didn't see him again until the night he died, and by the time we got there, he was a cold, waxy corpse.

The first dead person I ever saw was the shell of my grandpa.

He had loved me unconditionally, even when I was an ungrateful shit and didn't deserve it. The finality of all the bridges I could never build, the conversations we could never have, the questions I could never ask, the skills he could never teach me, hit me like a brick in the chest. I'm fairly certain none of that was on his mind that night, but in my self-centred teenage brain, it was the only thing on mine.

I struggled to be comforting to the grieving adults, because all I could focus on was how horribly I had failed at being a granddaughter and how I would never be able to make it up to him.

So, does the flowchart make any sense here?

Denial? I don't remember being in denial about him being dead, because I'd seen him and touched him and he was absolutely one hundred per cent dead. Did I go through denial about our relationship? I don't think so. I knew I was crying at that funeral over memories of him swimming with me, as a little girl, hanging onto his shoulders, and wishing I had been more like that little girl when I wasn't so little any more. I knew I was crying for myself as much as I was crying for the loss of him. I was self-centred, but not entirely blind to my faults.

Anger? I was plenty angry with myself for not making more of an effort before I went away, for not seeing my attitude of ennui as something that made *me* miss out and not the other way round. Okay, I probably didn't understand the ennui thing for another decade or so, but I was angry at myself. Was I angry at anybody else? I was filled with rage at the entire world at that point in my life, but I don't recall any of it being grief-related. It had been there before I went away and was fuelled by things that had nothing to do with my grandpa.

Bargaining?

The Flow Chart is Not For You

It was only at this point in writing the first draft of this chapter that I went and read more about those stages. As with so many things in life that you cannot understand until they happen to you, messages can become confused.

The flow chart isn't universal, it isn't necessarily about us, the ones left behind. It is based on the Kubler-Ross model and it was created as a framework to help people who have been given a terminal diagnosis who are trying to come to terms with their *own* mortality.

My mother is a great one for reading lots of books and doing lots of research. When she received her cancer diagnosis, she did the research and turned up for her appointment with the oncologist ready to quiz him on the components of the chemo cocktail he wanted to prescribe.

He wasn't expecting that.

When I was pregnant, she bought me a pile of books about pregnancy and parenting. They remained largely untouched. I have always been more of a go-with-my-gut girl.

When it came to Oliver's death, she didn't buy me any books. I don't know if she looked – I should probably ask her – but I know from the hunting I've done since committing to write this book that there weren't any.

There were no books that could help me to understand what I was feeling and how I was supposed to interact with a world that kept turning as if nothing had happened, or with the family members who were also grieving for Oliver in ways that sometimes clashed with mine.

There was nobody out there waving a flag for those grieving people with complicated and sometimes ugly relationships, saying, "It's okay, you're okay, it's all going to be okay."

Nobody wants to be that flag bearer. Believe me, I know. I never wanted to carry that flag, but my need to keep my head down is small compared to the need for forgiveness and unconditional acceptance that people need when this happens to them.

So, what is *your* sequence? And how long should it last?

Is there a deadline to how long you should grieve for a person who broke your heart and made you want to scream with sheer frustration while they were alive?

How about when you feel a glimmer of *relief* that your life will no longer revolve around *their* needs? Or that you will no longer have to walk on eggshells? Is there an accepted length of time before you won't feel a bit guilty about that glimmer of relief? Or for how long it will be before you can say out loud to another human being that you felt that way?

How long before *you* feel okay?

My pinball machine experience ricocheted between relief and guilt and self-loathing and relief and guilt and self-loathing and guilt and self-loathing and relief and guilt and relief and guilt and self-loathing more times than I can count.

It made my head spin and, at times, every molecule in my body hurt.

By sharing with you the sequence I have lived through, I hope that it will bring hope to you as you find your sequence. No two relationships are the same and I don't believe there is a simple flow chart that can bring comfort, especially for situations like mine or like yours.

What I do believe is that we can *all* move on from the darkness, through the shadows of half-light and into the sun.

I also believe that for some of us, the sun may feel warmer on our skin than it ever did before as we step out of the shadows.

Finding acceptance that your person is dead and not coming back is only the first step. The real work is in figuring out how you feel about it and about yourself.

Flow Charts and Feelings

When you feel ready, get out your journal. Write the question and then your answer.

1. Did I relate to the Kubler-Ross model?

2. Which bits made sense to me and which did not?

3. Who have I grieved for in the past, with whom I had an easier relationship than with the person I am grieving for right now?

4. Can I relate to stages that I have already moved through?

5. Do I relate to the feelings of relief?

    a. What are the things I feel relieved about?

    b. Does identifying them make me feel better?

6. What else do I feel at this point?

Circles of Trust

The concept of the Circle of Trust probably predates *Meet the Parents*, but Robert De Niro *is* the when, where and how it entered my life. It immediately made perfect sense to me. When De Niro is in the sheriff's cell arguing with Greg, he draws the Circle of Trust and places Greg outside of it. That moment became fundamental to the way I categorised people.

When you go through something as traumatic and destabilising as becoming a widow with a messy story, your circles of trust are vital. I have a lot of people in my life, and a lot of circles. I'm like a huge walking Venn diagram with lots of overlapping circles.

When you are falling, you learn who will reach out
to catch you.

When my best friend found out about Oliver's death, she offered to get on a plane with her baby and fly from America to be with me. You can't get much more caring than that.

A handful of close friends and family friends made the trek for Oliver's funeral, to make sure that I knew they had my back. Amy was one of them. She came down from London for the funeral and remains Tilly's Fairy Rock Mother.

I was surprised by many of those who came. I was even more surprised by those I reached out to who didn't come.

Building New Circles

But there was one group of people who really carried me through that first bit. Other than my parents, it was my NCT family. Oliver and I had moved down to Devon at the very earliest point at which I could start maternity leave. One of my senior managers told me that NCT friends would be essential to my survival as a new mum. My mum came with me to the classes, because Oliver had told me too many stories about his antics at antenatal classes he had attended with his ex.

In any case, between the first and second week of antenatal classes, I issued him with the ultimatum about going to rehab and he left.

I was nervous about saying anything because I wanted them to want to be my friends. But I blurted it out. Some stepped back and others stepped forwards. Tilly is nine years old and I am still in fairly regular contact with a few of them. Despite barely knowing me, they picked me up when he left. And they carried me when he died.

They made room for my darkness on countless little trips and meet-ups. Looking back, it reminds me of Eeyore's wonderfully glum pronouncements and how the gang always invite him to join them, no matter how miserable he's feeling.

None of my NCT buddies lived nearby. So, I had to go out and make friends without either them or my parents to hold my hand. This was a small, rural town with many lifelong and even inter-generational friendship groups, and I had to make friends in the midst of a massive identity crisis.

After Tilly was born, I went to baby groups because my mother told me I had to leave the house every day. I don't remember if she couched it as being about Tilly or not, but it was a clear directive that I had to go out. Their house, nestled in the middle of nowhere, was not conducive to long pram walks. There were too many hills and no footpaths. They gave me free access to a car and I used it to attend those playgroups, to meet up with the NCT girls and sometimes to simply go for a drive, find a place to sit and stare into space.

On the morning I received the news of Oliver's death, I had been speaking to another mum outside the baby group we both attended. I had complimented her on the perfect roundness of her daughter's head. She had smiled and made some comment about C-sections. Then we both got in our cars. I waited for the other cars to leave the car park before I picked up the phone and listened to the voicemail again. Then I dialled with shaking breath.

I knew what I was going to be told. I didn't want to hear the words, but I knew I was going to be told that he was dead.

I anchored myself in my new world by speaking to that mum before I dialled back to the old one where I had lived with Oliver.

That new mum was Sarah and, although she didn't know it, and certainly never asked for it, she became my anchor for quite some time after that. If she was in a room I walked into, I wanted to sit near her. She was my safe place. She didn't even have to speak to me; she just needed to be there like a life ring on a pier. She was always kind and seemed to know without asking that I was in a world of unrelenting pain.

She shared her friend circle with me. These were the friends she had made when she arrived as an outsider. She remains my friend today and I love her more than I can put into words.

One of the friends she shared with me was a doctor who let me rant and ramble as we went on walks on the moor. I don't know whether it was because she was a doctor and wanted to make sure my mental health wasn't deteriorating too much, or because she's one of the nicest people on the planet, but she must have spent hours just letting me download.

I swear a fair bit at the best of times, but I swore a lot in those hours. She waited until I was through the worst bits, probably a couple of years down the track, before she revealed that she can't bear swearing. She's an angel on earth.

Of course, there were times when Sarah wasn't there. I remember I walked into a baby group once, saw she wasn't there and nor was anybody else I recognised, so I went straight back to the car. Tilly was asleep, so we just sat in the car for an hour and then I drove home as if we'd spent the last hour in the suspended reality of that room.

Trying to make friends at that point in motherhood is like a school disco where you're on one side of the room and everybody else is on the other. You can make small talk about how little sleep you've had or how monumental the poop was or how weird certain things smell, but actually making *friends* is different.

As I've alluded to earlier when I discussed identity, in your ordinary life, you might never cross paths with the women you meet in a baby group, and yet, there you are, discussing your fears of prolapse or the potential for your nipple to actually come off altogether.

You can talk to the same woman in ten or fifteen different group settings without ever making the bold move of one of you asking the other out. It is basically, "Will you go out with me?" when you try to take a friendship beyond the surface level. It's bloody terrifying. I've talked about this with lots of friends who have been through this stage of motherhood at different times and in different places and it's pretty universal.

Added to that the grief void below my feet, I felt like Luke Skywalker in the core of the Death Star II in *Return of the Jedi*, knowing that if my foot slipped I could, like the Emperor, hurtle downwards into the nothingness.

I wasn't yet ready to have a conversation with *myself* about who I now was, let alone have that conversation with someone else. But I wanted to feel like I belonged somewhere. My gut instinct told me that having people I felt safe with would be a good start.

It is hard to put into words how grateful I am for my safe places. The people who met me as a complete mess and made me their friend are phenomenal humans. Not only did they accept me entirely at my worst, they celebrated my every small victory as I grew beyond the shadows and reached into the light.

I have built circles of trust in the darkest of times with people who will be my friends for the rest of my life.

None of this was how I would have expected it to play out. Very few of my London friends have been down to visit, but many have sent messages of love and support every year on the anniversary of Oliver's death. Whenever I let people know I am in London with an hour to kill, I find myself in joyous company. My circle waits for me, whenever I call upon it.

The Circle of Grief and the Importance of Personal Policies

Earlier, I wrote about the Circle of Grief, with its big circle of all the people who are living through grief and its smaller circle of the people grieving for the same person.

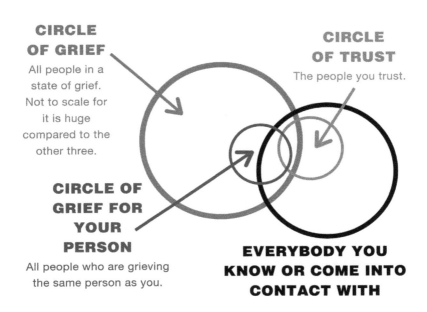

CIRCLE OF GRIEF
All people in a state of grief. Not to scale for it is huge compared to the other three.

CIRCLE OF TRUST
The people you trust.

CIRCLE OF GRIEF FOR YOUR PERSON
All people who are grieving the same person as you.

EVERYBODY YOU KNOW OR COME INTO CONTACT WITH

That circle can again be sub-divided into those who are in your circle of trust and those who are not.

Some societies, cultures and families have a very strong 'family first' attitude, encouraging family members to spend time with creepy uncles "because they're family".

Others have a slightly more relaxed approach where everyone is invited to weddings, christenings, funerals and Thanksgiving or Christmas, but there's no pressure to spend much more time together than that.

I have a personal policy around making my own decisions about people.

I have a personal policy about spending time with people I don't trust.

I have a personal policy about spending time with people I don't like.

I have a personal policy about spending time with people who drain me like energy vampires (or 'dementors' for those Harry Potter fans among you).

I have a personal policy about spending time with people who set my teeth on edge.

I have a personal policy about spending time with people who are bigoted and expect me not to challenge them on it, just because we are in some way related.

Thank you, Sarah Knight, for giving me the skills to frame my personal policies and the permission to speak them out loud. If you haven't read Sarah's book, *The Life Changing Magic of Not Giving a F**k*, it is well worth a read.

My father has always imbued in me the belief that worrying about what other people think is a waste of time and energy. I love him so much for this for, among other areas of my life, it made my teenage fashion experimentation way less stressful than many of my friends found it.

Family

I have a really wonderful family. I love most of them very much. They are a source of great pride and inspiration.

Oliver's family? Let's put it this way…he wasn't estranged just because of *his* behaviour.

While Oliver was alive, I only met a few of his family members, and many more have come into our lives since his death. Perhaps the fairest way to set the scene is to say that Oliver's decision about whether we should just throw ourselves into being in love and getting married and having kids from the outset was based on whether he thought I could handle his family. I should remind you that we didn't get married.

While he was alive, he was a buffer between what he did and did not want me to see of his family.

He told me about how proud he was of Melissa, the little sister he adored, how much he wished he could be more like Colin, her other half, and how difficult he found his relationships with his parents and twin brother.

Melissa and Colin

He introduced me to Melissa and Colin first, although none of us had any idea that that was his plan. We were out in the car with our dogs, probably on a tour of houses for sale, discussing the relative potential of each before deciding not to buy it. He directed me onto a road of very pretty houses and, as we pulled into one of the driveways, he announced that we were visiting his sister and her boyfriend. It would be safe to say that all three of us were caught off guard, while Oliver made himself a cup of tea and carried on as if we were all old friends!

He had told me many times before that he was sure his sister and I would get on, and that I would simply need to get through her layers of shyness first. He was entirely right. I now regard her as *my* sister – the one I always wanted but didn't get until I was in my late thirties. It didn't happen straight away though. I like to think that it evolved organically over time.

Over the seven years that Oliver and I were in and out of each other's lives, I crossed paths with Melissa and Colin several more times. There was the time we went to Guildford to walk the dogs and Oliver convinced Melissa to come out to her office car park to say hello, again without warning her that I was with him.

There was the time they were visiting him at his house on Hayling Island. He had invited me down but, once again, did not let either of us know about the other. You get the picture. I was never sure whether he did this to stop either me or Melissa from running away but, despite every meeting thrust upon us, I knew I liked her and hoped that she liked me.

Looking back, the breakthrough moment with Colin came on one impromptu visit to their house. Colin and I were alone in the living room and I asked him how, given his years of experience, he coped with having more than one Lund in the room at a time. He barely paused for breath and smiled, "Avoid ever having more than two in a room if at all possible and try to limit the time span to under half an hour." It proved to be sound advice.

I have always respected the fact that Colin's loyalty is steadfastly with Melissa, and that he didn't invest in the relationship with me until she was sure she wanted to. He will be the front man for as long as is necessary and he does it with more patience and diplomatic skill than most world leaders.

In the years immediately preceding Oliver's death, as he unravelled and disappeared into pain and prescription medication, he was sporadically unforgivably cruel to the ones he loved most. We would hurt less when he died, he claimed, if we could all just hate him a little bit. He was especially vicious with Colin and Melissa, sinking his teeth with extreme prejudice into their most painful vulnerabilities, quixotically, in my opinion, as I believe he loved them more than any of us.

When I saw them on the morning of his funeral, it was the first time we had been together in several months. The mood of devastation was lightened only by the presence of little Tilly, not yet three weeks old. We met in the car park and Melissa and I embraced.

The only time she'd hugged me before that day was months earlier, when we had last said goodbye.

That day, she had made a beeline for me and squeezed me tight, choking a "Thank you" into my hair. My eyes had filled up. I knew that no matter how much she and I wanted him to recover, our chances were slim at best.

In that second hug, on the morning of his funeral, I felt forgiven for failing.

It felt like a new beginning.

We got through the funeral and the wake, and a few weeks later we became friends on social media. A little while after that, she and Colin came down for Tilly's christening and then we started making plans to meet up, first, in places that were halfway between, and gradually progressing to staying with each other.

I didn't have a spare room in our first house, so they would stay in a local B&B. Once we moved and I made a point of setting up the spare room with a double bed and room for the dogs, they came to stay a lot. We quickly progressed to being comfortable watching TV in our pyjamas together, with Colin mowing my lawn and both of them cooking in my kitchen. My favourite Christmas in years was the one they spent with us. We try to see each other every couple of months and I remain extremely grateful that they do most of the driving and are the most helpful house guests imaginable.

My main fear in writing this book has been that I would upset our supremely supportive dynamic, and I hope that won't be the case.

His Family

My first encounter with Oliver's mother left me in tears. After that, I generally declined to get out of the car when he dropped in on her. I don't remember much of my first meeting with his twin, other than being slightly freaked out by this person who looked like Oliver, but who spoke with a broad Northern Irish accent. I remember their many sniping phone calls to each other, and some of the vile things he said about Oliver when I reached out for help.

I met my father-in-law, John, and his wife, Erica, at Oliver's funeral. I wish that had been our first contact, but there had been several terse and confrontational phone calls and emails in the year or so before Oliver's death. John's tone towards me had changed completely when Oliver told him I was pregnant. He actively sought a positive relationship with me, whether Oliver was involved or not. Naturally, I stuck by my man and refused to engage with his father while his relationship with Oliver remained so fractured.

Oliver's familial estrangement levels varied wildly and, by the time he died, he had largely cut himself off from everyone. Even though times were very tough in that last year of Oliver's life, I am a loyal creature, and would not reveal anything beyond what he wanted me to or what I felt was truly in his best interests. He had repeatedly insisted to me that I should have nothing whatsoever to do with his parents or his brother when he was no longer around.

Without him, in this new world where everything was blurry and Tilly was all I could focus on, I found myself without boundaries.

We all met before the funeral at a pub near the church – my parents, close family friends who had known Oliver, his parents, aunt, uncle and siblings – all thrust together in a series of fractured moments.

I tried to get Tilly to feed so that she would sleep through the service, but she was having none of it. Babies pick up on our tension, and I don't imagine I gave off any calming vibes that morning.

Before I knew it, we were getting back in the cars and heading for the church. Another family friend looked after Tilly at the back of the church during the service, so that I didn't have to walk in with the pram. Just me, in a place I'd last been with Oliver.

I couldn't figure out where I was supposed to sit, because nobody else was sitting down. I turned to my mother and she explained that they were all waiting for me to sit down, and then they would arrange themselves.

I didn't want to sit in the front row, so John and Erica sat in front of me and my parents, and more of my family and friends sat behind.

There was a moment during the service when I thought my legs were going to give way. Erica, who was standing in front of me, reached back without saying a word, and offered me a polo mint. She offered a crutch when I needed it most, and without expectation.

After the service, I followed the hearse on foot as far as I could. Then I watched it turn a corner and he was gone.

My father made it clear that we could leave if I wanted to. There was no expectation from my parents that I should stay for the wake but, if I wanted to, they would be there to support me.

I wanted to talk to Oliver's friends, but I had to get back to my baby. I especially wanted to talk to his friend from AA who I had called for guidance from a London bus when I was heavily pregnant.

I wanted him to know that he had given me solid advice and that Oliver, in saner days, would have agreed that I needed to concentrate on looking after myself and our baby.

But, by the time we got to the pub, his friends had all disappeared. They probably had jobs to get back to. Only Oliver's family remained. I had said I didn't want Tilly to be passed around, but she was taken from my arms and I only got her back when she was hungry. People took photos with her like it was some kind of happy gathering and not a sad day. I found that very hard to deal with.

I also found the 'we're all family' vibe very hard to deal with. It was surreal, bizarre, unfathomably weird. The fog of grief can be a real blessing. I was very happy to leave and drive away from that place and it took me years to go back and lay the ghost to rest.

When Oliver died, I had no reason to believe that I would build a relationship with anyone in his family. I wonder if they thought the same.

Colin and Melissa had bought a present for Tilly and, a year or so later, they told me that it had been a small thing because they didn't know if they would ever meet her. John made the grand gesture of inviting Tilly and me to go stay with him and Erica in Northern Ireland, as if that wasn't weird when we'd only just met.

Erica kept herself firmly in the background that day. She said she was the stepmother, so it wasn't her place to be front and centre. In reality, she loathed confrontation and knew from experience how bitchy Oliver's parents were to and about each other, despite having been divorced for twenty-five years. I think she also didn't want to form any attachment to Tilly in case the relationship was short-lived.

Over time, relationships have been invested in. I spent hours on the phone with John, who called regularly to get to know me and to assure me that he was in my corner. He said some things that sounded odd to my ears, but the intention was always good. Perhaps the most striking thing he said was on that first Christmas, barely seven weeks after Oliver had died. He said that he hoped I would meet somebody else and have more children. I know now that he was trying to tell me that he wanted me to be happy and not turn into Miss Havisham, but his delivery felt shocking, given that only a few weeks had passed since my world had been upended.

He loved that I was political, but we saw the world from diametrically opposing perspectives. He told racist jokes and seemed baffled when I didn't laugh. He thought a number of right-wing political personalities were wonderful but, when I told him what I thought of them, he would take a breath and change the subject. He knew I wasn't going to be swayed to his way of thinking and I think he respected that.

We were very different, but I never doubted that he loved me. Indeed, when I had to go to mediation with Oliver's ex and needed a support person, he insisted that he would be the one to share my pain. The stress made him horribly ill, but he simply repeated his personal motto, *Illegitimi non carborundum* – don't let the bastards get you down – and stayed resolutely by my side.

Erica, who at first needed coaxing to come to the phone, was initially reluctant to get involved. I think she'd been so hurt by questions from Oliver's ex about family money, that she wasn't sure she wanted to know me. I worked hard – that polo mint had been a lifesaver, so I knew there was a golden heart hidden in those skinny ribs. Once we had met up for a short holiday in Yorkshire, all reticence was swept aside. She and Tilly instantly became best friends, and she became one of my staunchest allies.

John's sister Liz and her husband have also been a wonderfully unexpected addition to our lives. Their kindness and generosity have meant the world to me and, along the way, they have become great friends to my parents. I am also hugely fond of their offspring, who I have bonded with at both Erica's and John's funerals. A family gathering that isn't around a funeral would be a nice change.

My personal policies have allowed me to spend time with the people I enjoy spending time with, and who I know care about us. My policies allowed me to have very different relationships with John and Erica than Oliver might have anticipated. Those policies have allowed me to get to know members of Oliver's family as people I like and would happily invite to a big birthday because I really want them to be there rather than because I feel any sense of obligation. The policies have also allowed me to filter who my daughter is exposed to and ensure that she only meets those members of his family who will add stability to her life.

My Circles of Trust

When you are ready, get out your journal. Write the question and then your answer.

1. Who is in my Circle of Trust?

2. Who is in my Circle of Grief?

3. Where do these two circles overlap?

4. With whom do I feel safe to share my feelings?

5. What are my personal policies about who I spend time with?

Crutches and Climbing Aids

I remember reading *We're Going on a Bear Hunt* with my baby perched on my lap and that line echoing around my skull. It is supposed to be a children's adventure story, but this insistence on the lack of alternative options, the "got to go through it" is what stayed with me. It is probably why I also didn't relish reading it when, as a toddler, Tilly chose it from the book box. Eventually, I put it out of reach so that I wouldn't have to read it any more.

The truth of it was irrefutable and at the time I didn't want to look at it.

The only way to go through grief is to go through it.

The only way to come out the other side is to go through it.

The only way to clear the decks and move forward is to go through it.

When the person or relationship you're grieving for wasn't all hearts and flowers, you know it's not going to be easy.

When the person you're grieving for died leaving unresolved anger or sadness between you, you know the regrets are going to be painful to face.

When the person you're grieving for ended their own life, or the death of that person actually gave you a sense of relief, the surge of guilt can be overwhelming.

When the last words you said to the person who died weren't "I love you" – well, nobody wants to relive that.

So, it really comes down to a choice of which is more painful. Is it worse to be stuck or to face it all?

For some people, this choice in itself seems just too hard. They are afraid to heal because their entire identity has been built around surviving the trauma they've experienced. They have no idea who they are outside of that trauma and the notion of being a survivor. Facing the unknown can be terrifying.

The way you perceive and tackle the obstacles in your path is not universal. It can be very frustrating to watch somebody look at what seems to be the same obstacle you're looking at and sail over it, while you're stuck, or lag behind as you resize it, step over it or crush it.

How bad can facing it all be? Worst case scenario, it can be pretty awful. But coming out the other side makes it all worth it.

Your crutches are those things you lean on to hold you up when you fear falling. And your climbing aids are what you use to pull yourself up from the bottom of the pit.

The Black Pit

I have been there, in that seemingly endless vortex of darkness. I have felt its gluey weight, dragging me ever deeper into the nothingness, where there is no light and no trail of crumbs to follow to get out.

I have heard the piteous whimpers and moans that snake through the silence, and not known if they have come from me. I have felt helpless in its grasp, defeated by its insidious omnipotence. I have given in to it calling me to unhook the lines of connection to the rest of the world.

But I fought my way out.

I didn't want to go there again.

I promised myself I never would.

And then Oliver died, and the black pit called to me again.

Much of the first year of Tilly's life was a blur of tears in the darkness. Night feeds with a chill in my bones that no fire could warm, my body wracked with silent sobbing while I tried to shield my newborn from the utter devastation I was struggling to process.

Baby groups where I would sit and say nothing because I was afraid that if I opened my mouth, the whole room would be filled with my grief and the joy would be sucked into the black hole inside me. The ugly snot face crying on my parents' kitchen floor when my baby slept and nobody else was home. The days when, no matter how much my hand shook, I applied make-up so that nobody who saw me would judge me as unfit.

I cried alone. I grieved alone.

I told myself I was holding it together in public. At home, I was exhausted, sleep deprived to my wits' end, struggling to care that I hadn't showered or eaten anything but custard creams in days. I worried that my baby was somehow absorbing my misery, because of all those things you read about babies being like little sponges. But, at the same time, I couldn't leave her alone in case she was taken away from me. In reality, there was never any danger of that, but it can be hard to be rational when you are that tired and your body is fuelled by tea and biscuits.

If you are in that place, or you are reading this to help somebody else who is, please know that it can get better. It gets better if you let it.

So how did I get out of that pit the first time?

The prescription medication route didn't work for me at all. Before I was prescribed them, I was struggling to watch TV without feeling sick when I saw people eating on screen. When I was taking them, I wanted to kill myself. I lasted a few days, scared the hell out of myself and my flatmates and then took them back to the GP. I was put on a waiting list for counselling, with the warning that there was a six-month waiting list to see someone.

I was at university at the time and I had broken up with my boyfriend. He was no ordinary boyfriend. He was the first guy I'd ever felt truly safe with. He accepted everything about me that I was willing to show him, he kissed my scars and told me that he loved me. We were both convinced that we had been in love for thousands of years and this was just the latest incarnation of our entwined souls. I could picture our children, hear their laughter and feel their embrace.

But nobody is perfect, and in this world most of the people I know are damaged, to some extent, by things that have happened to them in childhood. His way of acting out his damage was by cheating on girlfriends, including me.

He would explain that it was about feeling unworthy of me, and I didn't understand for a long time. I would forgive and try to forget. But one day, it all got too much and I told him I felt that he didn't love me any more. He didn't try to convince me I was wrong.

Suddenly my future, the picture that had been as clear as day in my mind for months, was crumbling and nothing was behind the façade. As my future with him disappeared, there was simply nothing in its place. It seemed that I had no future.

I don't remember the precise order of how things happened – a black veil clouds the memory, and everything was fuelled with booze. I know I hadn't slept for days and I'd taken to going running at three in the morning, partly because I was bored of pacing my room, and partly because I hoped I'd be murdered and wouldn't have to kill myself to end the pain.

I managed to get to my personal tutor's office. I had never met her before and I don't remember what I said, but she was kind to me and suggested I might want to take a break. She talked to all of my professors, made sure nobody would mark me down for not attending and asked the university's medical officer if she could help me access counselling any faster than the six-month waiting list my GP had put me on.

I called my parents in floods of tears. They told me afterwards that all they could decipher through the sobbing was "Come and get me or have me delivered in a box." My father said he would get in the car immediately. It was a four-hour drive from their house to my university, an eight-hour round trip. I could hear my mother saying to him, "But you've just got back, you're tired", and him saying that I needed him and he wouldn't forgive himself if I did something stupid just because he was tired. I said, "If I know you're coming, I can wait until tomorrow", and I started packing.

The next few weeks were spent going on very long walks with the family dog. Nothing soaks up tears the way dog hair does. We would walk and walk and walk and then sit down and he would lean against me with all of his weight, as if he believed that would make me feel more loved. He listened when I talked and let me be when I had nothing to say – my dearest friend and confidant.

There were chinks forming in the blackness now, areas of grey that had not been there before.

My parents also took me to see a chiropractor. I call him Magic Mr Booty. He assessed me physically, and made a few small adjustments. He also did some kinesiology, which was a new experience for me. Kinesiology addresses physiological, biomechanical, and psychological dynamic principles and mechanisms of movement. He told me to hold my arm out and resist him pushing down on it. Then he told me to think of a word and resist him again. Sometimes the strength went out of my arm as if it was made of candyfloss. Magic Mr Booty gave me the gift of sleep.

My parents also took me to a homeopath. I talked about how I was feeling and what haunted me and she gave me a remedy. The areas of grey were getting a little lighter.

Life Lines

The university medical officer contacted me, and asked me if I would like to see her while I waited for the appointment through my GP. It was a lifeline.

I went back to university, and went to see her. She invited me to talk and she listened. There was no time limit. I told her about being sexually assaulted as a child, fearing for my life and waking up in a white room thinking I was dead. I told her about being sexually assaulted again as a teenager, by somebody who was supposed to be a friend. I told her about being haunted by flashbacks through nightmares.

I told her about my self-destructive behaviour. I told her about my family and how I found it hard to talk to them about the sources of my pain because I didn't want them to ever feel that they had somehow failed to protect me. I told her about feeling like I had no future and how it made me want to die. I told her about what I had planned to do and what I had tried to do and how frustrating it was when I kept waking up in the morning.

She listened, without judgement. She simply sat quietly listening until I ran out of words.

Then she said, "I think it's a miracle you have survived this long. Maybe there's a reason for that?"

It derailed my train of thought about life simply being a one-way ticket to pain, pain and more pain. Maybe there was a reason? Maybe there was more to this than just punishing me for breathing? Maybe I wasn't simply working through the shitty karma of a previous life spent raping nuns or working for Hitler?

It took a bit longer for me to see that maybe the purpose of it all was to prepare me for what was yet to come, but she laid the foundations.

Not long before my world had imploded with that break up, I had made a new friend. Her name was Sara and she was one of the few who got in touch with me when I went home to my parents' house, checking to see that I was okay and asking if there was anything she could do to help out. Her simple act of getting in touch was more important than she will probably ever know in helping me make it back to university. She had very low expectations of me, so I didn't feel like a constant disappointment or walking failure when we spent time together.

The line, "When you can't see the light, I will sit with you in the darkness," reminds me of those times and that true friend.

She got me to leave the confines of my flat and even escorted me to a party hosted by one of my ex's best friends. We had agreed that we would go for the start of the party and my ex would go for the second half. There was a legendary moment at that party, however, when he arrived a bit earlier than anticipated, with another girl clinging to him.

My friend twirled me around on the dancefloor so that my back was to him and said, "I'd be less shocked if my leg fell off right now, than I am at how ugly that bird is." I laughed. I laughed so hard our hostess came to check I was okay. I told her what my friend had said and she laughed too. We left the party without drama and I knew that Sara would be my friend for the rest of my life.

So, I had a family who loved me, someone to talk to, who listened without flinching and I had a friend who made me laugh again.

I was lucky to have them, but the hard work was mine.

Turning Point

There was a turning point, when I decided I was bored. Depression is so fucking boring.

I love this quote and, sadly, I don't know the source.

"The Devil whispers 'you can't withstand the storm' and the warrior whispers back 'I am the storm'."

I wish I could say that my life was poetic and dramatic like that. But it was simply a chat in the mirror. It went along the lines of, "Fuck this shit. They did the crimes, why the fuck should I do the time?" I made a decision to live.

At that age and stage in my life, my interpretation of what that meant was different to what it means now, but the key part was that I didn't want to die any more.

"Maybe there's a reason?" started to have meaning for me.

I began to remember times from the past when seeing the silver linings of dark clouds had helped me.

Before going to university, I had worked for three years. During that time, I was able to offer a worried father some insight into why his suicidal teenage daughter couldn't talk to him. She had been through a similar childhood experience as me, at a similar age, and was struggling to escape the flashbacks and nightmares. It was spoken of in hushed tones by the handful of people who knew what was going on. I still wonder why the person who told me this girl's story chose to take me into the circle of trust, but I'm glad they did.

I sat down with that father one lunchtime and tried to explain that his daughter's inability to talk to him was actually a sign of how much she loved him, and that she was trying very hard to protect him from feelings that would cause him suffering – guilt that he hadn't protected her and rage over what had been done to her. I assured him that I was fine and that she would be too, as long as she got the help she needed and the space to process. I hope she made it.

I started looking for the silver linings and developed a faith around their existence. Sometimes they can be very, very elusive, but they are always there if you just look hard enough.

I was patched up and ready for my next adventure.

Patched up was the best I thought I could hope for, as how could I undo the things that had been done to me? How could

I un-experience the darkness? There is no cure for the condition called 'life experience' is there?

A few years down the line, I needed help again. This time, I found a different kind of help, a different kind of work and a different kind of result.

Crutches

What comes to mind when you hear the word 'crutches'?

I don't know why, but my thoughts always go straight to movie versions of *A Christmas Carol* and Tiny Tim Cratchit limping around with an old wooden crutch. Then I think of the cool kids at school who broke legs skiing or falling out of trees and the way they used crutches to fly down corridors. I've had the metal version, after a car accident in 2007. I only got one, though, because I'd broken my collarbone as well as my ankle. So, there was no supercool flying down corridors for me, just lopsided leaning.

Without the crutch, I could hobble a few steps if necessary, but I was frightened to go any further without it to help bear my weight. It had a very real physical purpose, but its mental purpose was even more important. Having that crutch made me believe I could do more.

Having that crutch made me believe I could walk the dog around the park.

Having it made me more confident to walk to the supermarket and get provisions.

Having it was a vital component of me learning to walk again and, eventually, even to run.

However, we all use other things as crutches to lean on, don't we?

Some of us use people to lean on, maybe our family, best friend or spouse. At times, being Oliver's crutch took over my life. I wrestled with friends' accusations of co-dependency, and that was definitely one aspect of it. If it's new to you, co-dependency means that one person in a relationship can only feel okay if the other person feels okay. Given that his pain and medication cocktail left him prone to mood swings, unpredictable behaviour and talk of ending everything, our co-dependency was possibly a more forgivable form than simply being obsessed with another human. It was exhausting.

Thank you from the bottom of my heart to all of the people who have been my crutches.

Some of us use other things, like food. There are numerous social norms around the food crutch. If you've had a horrible break up, you'll be expected to eat a tub of ice cream in front of the TV. When you're on a diet as part of a dieting club, you often have a big meal after weigh-in. My bestie and I called it the "points void" and looked forward to the end of each diet week and that one big meal that got us through the less exciting days of jacket potatoes without butter or cheese.

Custard creams were my crutch of choice for quite some time. When Tilly was about five months old, she and I had moved into a rented house. I rarely had more than one hand available, as she always wanted to be cuddled and held and not left behind. I could make tea one handed. I could eat biscuits one handed. I could focus for three or four glorious seconds on scraping the creamy sugary glue bit off the biscuit with my teeth and then four or five more in letting it melt on my tongue.

I gave up smoking when I had the positive pregnancy test in my hand. I'd been smoking for twenty years, punctuating social moments by sparking a fag and taking a long drag as I figured out what to say or tried to look alluring.

I smoked when I was bored.

I smoked when I wanted to change the topic in my head.

I smoked when I cooked.

I smoked when I drove.

I smoked when I wanted peace.

I smoked when I wanted company.

I smoked a lot.

I'd tried to quit a few times but I didn't know how to navigate life without smoking. What did people do when they were waiting for somebody if they didn't smoke? How did you have an awkward conversation without those wonderfully useful pauses injected by the need to light a cigarette or take a really deep drag?

These were the gaps that biscuits filled the best. When I found out that it wasn't frowned upon for a breastfeeding mother to have a whole packet in her change bag, I ate them out and about too. I ate them when I made a cup of tea, I ate them when I watched TV, I ate them when people came around, I ate them alone, I ate them instead of lunch and sometimes dinner. I ate them a lot.

I'm glad I found biscuits and didn't take up smoking again.

Having largely put down the biscuits now too, writing this has made me miss them terribly! That is the power of our minds' connection to our chosen crutches.

Alcohol

Alcohol is another crutch I leaned on and hid behind for many years. Have you ever wanted to do something a bit daring but not felt you could without some 'Dutch courage'? Have you ever spent a night out doing things you wouldn't do without being drunk? Has someone ever said to you at the end of a hard day that you should put your feet up and have a gin? Or open a bottle of red wine? Have you ever drunk to cushion your ears from how dull the company is? How about to help you relax? Or just to numb the pain?

My family had a horrific 2007. There was my car accident, Mum and Dad had the house sale from hell, and then bought a money pit, our dog Mackie died suddenly, and Mum was diagnosed with cancer.

Mackie's death hit me very hard. It wasn't just that he was a great dog. He'd been my counsellor and confidante during the great breakdown at university and he'd been the one who got me out of bed after the car accident. I felt I literally owed him my life. I hadn't said goodbye. My best friend was gone and I hadn't been there to tell him how much I loved him, I hadn't told him what a good boy he was and I hadn't given him his last cuddle. My mum called to let me know that he was gone.

I couldn't breathe for the sobs wracking my body. I stumbled down the stairs to the window where my flatmate let me smoke and I cried silently. I felt like I couldn't walk. My canine crutch had been stolen from me. My smoking crutch wasn't helping, so I walked to the shop and bought a bottle of wine. This is the blessing and curse of living in the centre of any town or city – many of your crutches are available on your doorstep. Living in central London, fuelled by that relentless shitstorm of a year, my drinking spiralled out of control.

Hiding in the bottle meant numbing my pain, quietening the spinning voices of doom in my mind and convincing myself that my mum wasn't potentially going to die. It made a lot of sense. I had hidden in the bottle sporadically over the years and it had always done its job.

Or so I thought.

The following Christmas, I was determined to make a trip home to Australia without alcohol. I was on a holiday between jobs and I didn't want to start my management role in the new company with a drink in my hand. I failed miserably and drank at my cousin's wedding in Canberra. So, I tweaked the goal to not drinking in New Zealand. Then I drank at my cousin's birthday in Christchurch. I couldn't seem to say no to it. I wanted to be the life and soul of the party and I felt like I had to drink to be interesting.

Oliver was a chronic alcoholic. He had been upfront with me about it early on. He was in recovery when we met, so I didn't see or hear him drunk. He had asked me about my drinking habits and when I asked him if he thought I had a problem, he said I was probably fine, but that I should always remember that AA was there for everyone who wants help with their drinking.

Oliver and I weren't even talking to each other when I did the online quiz for the fifth time and decided I really couldn't fight it any more.

In a bar one night, I had an epiphany while surrounded by my work colleagues. I was fucking this job up just like I had the one before. I was a caner in the eyes of my team, something I might have relished when I was younger, but not now. My drinking was getting in the way of my life. I had failed miserably at trying to control it, so I needed to stop altogether.

I thought AA would be about the practicalities of how to not drink. Things like how to get around toasts at weddings without attracting attention to the fact you're not on the champagne. And while there were some helpful practical tips, AA was about so much more.

It takes a while for the key messages to sink in, so a lot of them were repeated at the meetings and in the coffee shops where we hung out afterwards. For me, the most powerful message was that having the 'ism' isn't about what you drank, when you drank or how much you drank. It is about *why* you drank. I Sabotage Myself. ISM. If you drink to change how you feel, you may well share this malady.

The good news is that there's this phenomenally successful programme called the Twelve Steps that has been saving people from self-destruction all over the world for more than eighty years. The Twelve Steps programme taught me about the vital importance of facing my demons, resizing them and letting them go. Living in the day isn't just a catchphrase, it is a method for living.

The Truth Will Set You Free

One key aspect of the programme is being brutally honest with yourself and another human being about your resentments, including the things that haunt you.

In Step Four, we were invited to make a thorough inventory of ourselves. This is almost always written down. My sponsor was very, very thorough. She also made a lot of time for me. My Step Four work filled a lever arch file and it took us five full days to go through it all. It was so thorough that I felt entirely better about myself and my life when we finished.

Oliver was horrified by the prospect of having to complete Step Four thoroughly enough that it would help him stay sober long term. Not only did he have the normal fear of not wanting to drag everything up and lay it out in the open, he was paralysed by the idea of having to *write* it. He was chronically dyslexic. In his work life, he had relied heavily on having a secretary or office manager to take dictation. There was no one he trusted to dictate this stuff to who wouldn't be hurt by it to some extent.

Over time, as I learned more about his formative years, I came to understand that he'd been threatened so many times with dire consequences if he ever told anyone about the abuse that he'd been subjected to that, even as an adult, he was terrified to try. Not completing his Step Four meant that he never completed his steps and, thus, never achieved true recovery.

Russell Brand's fabulous book, *Recovery*, takes the reader through the steps as they relate to all types of addictive behaviour. I thoroughly recommend getting the audiobook too, so you can listen to him and highlight the bits of the book that speak to you. He swears a lot, but it's a great way to access the programme if the religious element of the original literature is not for you.

The Gift of Sobriety

I fulfilled my lifetime drinking quota a few years before Oliver died, so I grieved for him sober. His loss has been one of the most painful because of our daughter. But my ability to cope has been profoundly more manageable because of my sobriety.

I don't believe that anyone is born to be an addict. I believe your genes may make you more predisposed to it, but far more depends on your environment and life experiences. A key factor is whether or not you grow up feeling good enough. It is a huge bonus to be blessed with parents who do everything in their power to make you believe that you are, in fact, good enough. But it's not always enough.

I have talked to people who, just like Oliver, have ricocheted in and out of recovery for decades. And I have talked to people with thirty years of recovery to share, who walked into their first meeting in their teens and never looked back.

I used to say to Oliver, "Recover or die, there is no third option", and I think grief is exactly the same. We must recover or we wither inside under the weight of our trapped emotions.

Recognising the crutches you use and whether they are enabling you to get up from the pit, find the path and take your first steps towards the sunshine, is a powerful part of deciding to move out of the darkness.

Climbing Aids

My climbing aids are my lifestyle, my family and my friends.

What do I mean by 'my lifestyle'? Having been through a very rigorous process of facing all of my old demons, I can deal with what happens to me in the moment. I don't hide from my feelings and I don't carry emotional baggage the way I used to. That's not to say that I always win at expressing my feelings – it can take me a while to process them because I want to know that I have understood them before I give them airtime, but it does mean that I'm much less likely to have to backpedal. The people in my life know that I say what I mean and I mean what I say.

I also make a point of looking after both my physical and mental health on a daily basis. I take proactive responsibility for my self-care. I go outside for a walk every day – dogs are great for this –

and spend as much time in nature and around trees as I possibly can. I make sure that I have creative time in my life – ceramics, crafting, painting, sewing and writing – and I am learning to meditate.

And I have my unshakeable belief that I can find meaning in anything that happens to me. As for crutches, I'm not afraid to fall any more. I still eat biscuits sometimes, but I no longer carry a packet in my bag.

Horrible and devastating things happen to good people all the time. We are not in control of those things, but we can control how we respond to them.

My Crutches and Climbing Aids

When you are ready, get out your journal. Write the question and then your answer.

1. Am I holding my own weight right now?

2. When I feel like I can't, who do I lean on?

3. When there is no person to act as my crutch, what do I turn to?

4. How do my crutches support me?

5. How do my crutches delay my recovery?

6. Have I been in the darkness before?

7. What tools can I use to help me pull myself out of the darkness?

8. Do I need help finding the tools or learning how to use them?

Anniversaries

I am writing this on anniversary number seven. Seven whole years. But we'll get to that in a bit.

We all have to get through the first anniversary first. The first year is a blur of tears in the darkness.

At times, all those 'firsts' seemed to stack on top of the other. I have a fridge magnet, which long predates being widowed, that sums up a lot of that first year for me.

'I try to take one day at a time, but sometimes several days attack me at once'.

I met so many people for the first time with whom I then had that awkward chat where they got this look in their eyes as if they'd put their whole body in their mouth by asking about Tilly's dad. I felt as if I had to counsel them, to make them feel better. I couldn't lick my wounds with an audience, so I would save up the picked emotional scabs until I was at home and everyone was asleep, and then the floodgates would open.

Tilly was born in October, Oliver died ten days later and his funeral was on 11.11.11. The congratulation cards were mingled with the sympathy cards, and I didn't know which way was up – an emotional rollercoaster greased with a new mother's cocktail of hormones.

When Christmas rolled around, I was still in the shock phase. It all seemed very, very surreal.

The previous December we had argued over whether he was coming to my parents' house for Christmas. He decided to come in the end, and I'm glad, because he said it was, without question, the best Christmas he'd ever been part of, surrounded by people who genuinely loved each other and were willing to share that circle with him.

It was a white Christmas, and we had a fairly hairy drive across the south coast on roads covered in slush, the headlights catching the snowflakes as they fell on the road in front of us.

We went for a walk with the dogs in the woods behind my parents' house on Christmas Eve, and Mum sent my Dad out with the camera. It felt a bit weird, but I'm so glad now that he did the paparazzi routine and took lots of photos of us. I now cherish that collection of pictures of us in the snow, laughing, holding hands, trying to look very *Downton Abbey* dignified and then playing like kids.

I took a video of him playing in the snow-covered garden with Mr Wiggles the dog, but my phone was a basic model and there is barely any sound. I watched it over and over and over.

The prospect of my first Christmas with a baby, but without him, in the same house, without him, was frightening. I had always loved Christmas but now it would be sad because it would be without him. A year since we'd been here together and we'd been so happy. But now...

The tension built inside me. I was so frightened of what Christmas Day would be like and how much it would be ruined by him being dead.

I don't remember now if I crumbled on the way, but I know I went out on Christmas Eve with my baby, and I came home with her fast asleep. I carried her into the house in her car seat and put it down safely. Nobody else was in the house, and the dam burst.

My legs gave out and I was a sobbing mess on the kitchen floor, full-blown ugly crying with snot everywhere that I didn't even notice because all I was aware of was the pain, the great chasm of pain and loneliness and sadness inside me that threatened to swallow me, and I let go and gave in and cried and sobbed and howled.

Tilly slept peacefully, blissfully unaware.

My parents came home and found me in that state, unable to speak or move, my whole body wracked with sobs so hard they had no sound. I didn't want to share this with them, to make them see how bad it was, to make them feel bad, but I was beyond hiding by then.

Eventually the storm passed.

I finally felt how cold the floor was. I picked myself up, hugged my parents, washed my face and carried on parenting.

In the end, Christmas Day itself was fine, with just the one sad blip when Dad made his usual toast to absent friends.

I started to learn something hugely valuable from that experience.

Until you have been there, it is hard to imagine. There's this build up in advance when, whether you consciously know it or not, you're frightened of how cataclysmically bad THAT DAY is going to be. It doesn't matter if it's Christmas, or their birthday or your anniversary or THE anniversary. It's just something that happens inside you.

I understand now that it was anticipatory anxiety but, at the time, I was just frightened, terrified of the unknown and I attached that fear to specific dates. Maybe doing that made the other days in between easier to face, because they weren't THAT DAY. I don't know. But it's a coping mechanism for which I grew immensely grateful.

His birthday was tough, and I refused to start our planned family holiday that day because it didn't feel right to go on holiday without him on his birthday.

Next was the first anniversary of his death. I had resisted pressure to do anything with his ashes that day. Oliver's father was stalwart in his support of me as sole beneficiary of the will and insisted it was my call as to what happened to Oliver's remains. I will be forever grateful for John's support.

The anticipatory thing happened again and, had it not been for the people in the world who didn't know or give a crap about my life or the significance of it being the night before THAT DAY, I might have been okay.

He died on 1 November, so the night before THAT DAY, the biggest of THAT DAYs that I had faced so far, people dressed as the undead kept banging on my front door for sweets. They were there because people knew I had a kid, our bathroom light was on, shining over the front door, and my car was in the drive. They were trick-or-treating and I was giving Tilly a bath before heading to bed and hiding. When they rang the bell again or hammered harder on the door, I wanted to open the window and yell down at them all to fuck off and die.

I've never been a Halloween person anyway but, that night, I hated it and everything it stood for. The world is full of people who don't know or care about your private stories of grief or your significant dates. They go on living every day out there without stopping to honour your loss.

In that moment, it can be hard to see that you are also carrying on living your life, oblivious to the pain and loss that other people are feeling. None of us is alone in feeling this way, but it truly feels the loneliest.

I got Tilly out of the bath, turned off the light, and dressed her for bed by the light of my phone. I told her a story rather than trying to read one in the dark, and I curled up beside her until she slept.

Then I went into the other bedroom and took out my iPod. I listened to our songs – Snow Patrol's *Chasing Cars*, James Blunt's *You're Beautiful* and *Goodbye My Lover*, Katy Perry's *Firework* and yes, I'm pretty sure I also cried through *I Will Always Love You*. I cried and I cried and I cried and I hid from the world while my baby slept.

The next day, the actual THAT DAY of the first anniversary of Oliver's death, was nowhere near as bad as I had feared. It was a bit of an anti-climax. Then I beat myself up for not feeling worse on THAT DAY as if it somehow diminished how much I loved him.

It's all bollocks of course. You feel sad when you feel sad. You feel not sad whenever you can, unless you have convinced yourself that if you don't feel sad all the time then you're kidding yourself and everybody else about how much you loved him. Guilt in grief is so toxic. Most of it is internal dialogue, and that is bad enough.

Some of it comes from people projecting onto you their own guilt about how they feel or how they don't feel and how they think they *should* be feeling. They are simply trying to distract attention from themselves and their own perceived inadequacies.

Confusing? Did you need to read that again?

Because the people who are raging outwardly and judging your grieving process are probably very messed up inside and really struggling. Be kind, and if you can't be kind, walk away.

I don't remember the specifics of the other anniversaries, but my coping mechanism for all of the emotion that builds inside me and the busyness of being a single parent and self-employed and trying to spin all of the plates all of the time has remained the same. After that first anniversary, I made myself a promise. Until the end of time, I am allowed to cry and rage and be as emotional as I want on the night before his birthday, the night before the anniversary and on New Year's Eve. If I ever fall over Prince Charming, his acceptance of this will be key to knowing that he's the right one.

That's not to say that I rage and ugly cry every year on those three nights, because I don't. But I am allowed to, so my inner Pandora's Box knows exactly when it is safe to open the door.

I plan work and holidays accordingly, so that I can hold my shit together for the other 362 days and nights of the year.

On the night before the sixth anniversary, I didn't feel like crying, so I made my vision board and felt awesome. On the night before the seventh I did a few rounds with Mike Tyson, or so my body told me in the aftermath of a truly gut-wrenching night of emotional download.

You can't predict the rate at which you will feel better, or if it will be a smooth trajectory. But you can be kind to yourself and create some boundaried time in which to let it go.

I wholeheartedly recommend making a playlist of 'your songs', so that on those nights when you are free to release, it is easy to open the door.

My Anniversary Plan

1. Be kind to yourself.

2. Give yourself two or three designated days or nights to get off the hamster wheel of life *every year* and to simply feel and cry and release. This has kept me going and enabled me to grow over the past nine years. I wholeheartedly recommend it.

3. Plan ahead

   a. Book time off work or speak to your manager to explain that you may need to take a personal day.

   b. If you have time freedom, plan something nice to do, whether it is doing something that 'honours' the one who is gone or something that is one hundred per cent about something *you* like.

    c.   Ringfence that time so that you don't have a deadline to meet, a child's birthday party to organise or a speech to give at a wedding.

4.   If music is anywhere near as powerful for you as it is for me, set up your playlist so that when you have a safe space and feel the need to release, you can open the floodgates with ease.

5.   If you have a special movie, make sure you have a copy of it to hand. If you don't have one, I offer you *Me Before You*, which is hard to watch without crying.

6.   Embrace the fact that it won't all be over in a year. The first anniversary is one of the hardest, but you will continue to have feelings for years to come. Some people will remember the first anniversary without being told, few will remember any subsequent year. If you want to do an anniversary post on social media for the rest of your life, go right ahead. If you don't feel like it every year, then don't feel you ought to. Your grief is yours, and it's your right to share it only if and when *you* want to.

7.   When you feel ready, get out your journal. Write an anniversary entry. As you may have noticed, I sometimes write poems. They help me to get out what is in my head and my heart. I don't care if other people think they're 'good' or not. They are my therapy and I feel lighter when I finish one. You may wish to share what you write, or you may not. Trust me when I say that you will look back on those entries in years to come and they will help you to see your progress.

8.   If you're really struggling, you may wish to skip forward to what I wrote in the *New Beginnings* chapter in Part Four. Like I said, it gets better if you let it. xx

Signs

I am not religious, but I am spiritual and I believe in signs.

I believe they are there for all of us, sometimes we just need to open our eyes or hearts to see them.

I also believe we are shown what we most need, when we most need it.

These are a few of my most memorable signs. If nothing else, some of them might make you smile.

The Vestry

As the funeral came to a close, and Oliver's coffin was being loaded into the back of the hearse, I realised I was never going to be near him again. I am choking up even as I write these words, all these years later. The finality of it all started to sink in at that moment and, while I followed on foot, I could still see the edge of his coffin and then the hearse went around the corner and he was gone forever.

I was struggling for breath and then my eyes focussed on Mike, one of Oliver's wonderful friends from AA and I had oxygen again. I didn't see him before or after that moment, only at the exact time when I needed to feel anchored to something safe.

I can't remember if someone came to get me or if I just knew, but I had to run back to the church to where Tilly was crying her heart out. She was not quite three weeks old and had been at the back of the church for the duration of the ceremony with a family friend.

My mum took us into the little vestry that was more used to being used for church flowers and I got out the change mat and laid it on the table, with Tilly on it. I undid her clothes and…if you're squeamish, skip the next bit, okay?

I took off her nappy and there was a veritable river of poo. I couldn't catch it in the nappy and there was a frantic cry for something to catch it, a bucket, anything. The verger produced a bucket and suddenly we were crying with laughter. My baby had produced a once in a lifetime poo river, right at the time when I most needed to laugh.

When I looked back on it afterwards, I remembered Oliver telling me the story of accompanying his dear friend Mo to her father's funeral. To break the tension, he and Mo's ex-husband had been teasing her that she looked as if she really needed a shag. Chronic inappropriateness was one of the most entertaining, embarrassing and unpredictable elements of Oliver's character. Somehow the incident in the vestry was just that. It set me up to survive the wake just as surely as if he'd been there, cracking inappropriate jokes.

The Number Plate
It was a month or so later and I was in the car with Tilly, driving back to my parents' house, and my mind was going around in circles about

Oliver and my identity as a widow and how to explain how he died and so many other things. And then the radio cut through my mental chatter. Our song was playing – Snow Patrol's *Chasing Cars*. We used to sing it together in the car. And here I was, in the car, with our song playing and our baby in the back and for a moment I felt like he was beside me in the passenger seat singing that final poignant verse to me. But we both choked on that final line about how nothing would change. Because everything had changed, hadn't it?

I was consciously breathing deeply to stave off the tears when the next song started. It was Adele singing Make You Feel My Love and it simply couldn't have been more perfectly or lethally timed. I was beginning to lose my battle with the tears as Adele reminded me that I would be crying alone. Then, as I was waiting to make a right turn, I saw that the number plate on the car coming towards me was OV10LND. I was glad I wasn't in motion as I think I would have gone off the road. I pulled over and had a cry before attempting the final mile. I felt so held by him, so reassured that he knew I had done my best and that I loved him and that he loved me.

I saw that same car again a year or so later when I was having a tough time letting go of something. It lifted my spirits. I haven't seen it again in the years since. I see that as a sign too.

Innocence

A few months later, my father helped me to clear out Oliver's house. I had waited several months, partly because of the practicalities of having a tiny baby and partly because I didn't want to go there. I didn't want to be in the place where *we* died, the place where he died.

I was still breastfeeding at the time, so I had been pumping like a dairy cow for a couple of weeks beforehand to make sure Mum would have enough to keep Tilly happy while we sorted and packed. I also needed to stop and pump during the day to keep my supply up. As anybody who has been involved in pumping knows, it's really hard to get the desired result if your heart's not in it.

So, there I was, in this shell of a half-renovated house, with Oliver's half-rolled cigarettes still on the kitchen table, the microwave perched on the Black & Decker workmate in the corner, the dishwasher still half full of mouldy crockery. I was struggling. It was a sad house to begin with and the air of melancholy never quite lifted. Dad was in the garage trying to give me some space and nothing was flowing but tears. I looked out the window towards the mud of low tide and saw a movement out of the corner of my eye. From under a bush at the edge of the garden appeared three fox cubs, in broad daylight. They wrestled, chased their tails and played there for about twenty minutes.

Dad walked into the living room, almost silently, and I signalled to him to move slowly and look out the window. He saw the young foxes playing too, and it gave both of us the light relief we needed to keep going for the rest of the day.

The absence of human life in the house had allowed wildlife to flourish – the closing of one door had opened a new one. I completed my task with ease as I watched them frolicking, their joyous innocence making it feel as if the sun had come out from behind the clouds. I think of him whenever I see foxes, particularly when they are gadding about in semi-urban areas.

The House

A couple of years later, when I started house hunting, I began the process with no real idea of my budget. I tried to envisage myself and Tilly living in these houses and playing in these gardens that belonged to other people and none of them ever felt quite right. One day, a new listing popped up. It was a shell of a house in a village with no facilities that was closer to my parents but further from my friends. It didn't have gas central heating and was unlikely to have superfast internet. The carpets were threadbare and it needed a new kitchen and bathroom, and the garage needed to be converted. I didn't want a building project, but felt drawn to go see it anyway.

When I went out in the 'garden' – a big expanse of overlong matted grass in desperate need of mowing – there was a small cluster of red poppies by the back fence. I saw this as his nod to me that I should buy the house, so I did. Oliver was passionate about poppies and the Poppy Appeal. The November before I was pregnant, he had turned a quick trip to Asda into an hour-long performance while he made every person leaving the supermarket buy poppies from the unsuspecting volunteers.

It's not a perfect house, but living here has led me to finding one of the most wonderful and inspiring friends a person could ask for. Those poppies have never appeared again in the six years since that day, and I see that as a sign too.

The Ashes

Hmmm *ashes to ashes, dust to dust*. Until you have experienced human ashes, you might expect, as I did, that they would have the consistency of dust.

Spoiler – they don't.

I was the sole beneficiary of Oliver's will. As such, Oliver's father was of the opinion that his mortal remains should also be mine to do with as I saw fit. Sadly, Oliver's family was not unified in that belief, but once John had asked the funeral director to release the ashes to me, it was no longer anybody else's decision.

The ceremonial bits of a person's death must be carefully managed. The desires of the person who has died must be balanced with the desires of those left behind. The funeral was organised without me, and while, at the time, I felt tiny glimmers of confusion about why I wasn't asked to be more involved, I was mostly grateful, as I'm not sure if I'd have been any use at all. When it came to the ashes, however, I was in charge.

I felt from the outset that Oliver's ashes should wait until his faithful sidekick was ready to join him. Mr Wiggles, Russian Migs, Professor Wigglemunch, Wigglebum, or Tigger as he was officially known, was Oliver's best friend. I had never known Oliver without him and the two were as inseparable as any human-canine combination can be. Wiggles surprised us all by living at least a year longer than anyone expected. Quitting his smoking habit and taking up walking and good food probably had a good deal to do with that (thank you Colin and Melissa).

His extended time on earth made refusing the "it should be on the first anniversary" request from elsewhere in the family relatively easy. It was difficult for anyone who knew Oliver to deny that he'd want to be with his dog in the hereafter. I thought it also meant I could put off thinking about the where and the how and the when, until Wiggles had also moved on.

I was wrong, but it was a nice thought while it lasted! It came up in conversation with John and I could tell it was something he needed a resolution for.

I explained that Oliver had been pretty clear about cremation because he didn't want anybody to visit a grave. I think I told John and Erica that Oliver didn't want me feeling tied to living in a place within visiting distance of his grave.

However, what Oliver had actually said was that he didn't want a grave that people would visit, where they could pretend that their relationship with him in life had been anything more than it was, or where they would weep and apologise for having behaved so badly.

If his ashes were scattered on land, it would have to be somewhere high where the wind would carry them and there wouldn't be some chunk of him left in one place. Had it not been for the fact that Wiggles hated fireworks, I would absolutely have sent them up in one because Oliver loved them, and it was one of our songs.

Scattering his ashes at sea seemed to be a clear winner. Oliver had rarely looked or sounded more gleeful than when describing his shenanigans with catamarans and sailboats, and he'd always wanted to travel the world. John and Erica approved, and when I discussed it with Colin and Melissa, they seemed pretty happy with the idea.

I had seen enough comedy sketches of people ending up covered in the ashes of their loved one when the wind changed during an open scattering to know I didn't want that. I sourced a beautiful bio-degradable urn decorated with poppies, that could be dropped into the water with its lid sealed. Over time, the urn would bio-degrade and the ashes would be distributed by the currents.

I found a boat with a skipper who was experienced in this kind of trip. I explained the family politics that might or might not play out on his boat and I made the booking. Seats were limited to six so I invited family members only.

With my heart in my mouth, I emailed invitations to Oliver's parents, brother, sister, and brother-in-law. His brother replied swiftly, saying that he wouldn't be able to make it. His mother phoned to berate the plan, leaving me no option but to eventually hang up on her.

Tilly went to my parents for her first two-night sleepover and I drove across the south coast. I stayed with my best friend, who was briefly stationed in the area. I got up on the morning in question and drove to the village where his funeral had been. It was the first time I'd been back since that day.

The vast majority of Oliver's and Wiggle's combined ashes were safely in the poppy urn, waiting to go on the boat.

I had poured some water into the big plastic urn Oliver had arrived in, as I didn't want bits of him left in there to be sent off to a recycling plant. It meant I had dregs to find a home for.

No matter my opinion of her, she was his mother and if having a place to visit on land was that big of a deal for her, the dregs would be put somewhere specific for that purpose. So I grabbed the very unsubtle big red plastic urn and headed into the village to look for somewhere to subtly tip them out for her. I hovered in the churchyard, trying to be discreet while I looked at the green beyond.

I had imagined that I could sit on a bench and quietly tip the grey liquid contents of the urn out beside me without attracting any attention. But every flipping bench was occupied.

As I sighed and tried to think of a Plan B, I was spotted by the vicar, who clearly thought I was trying to scatter the entire contents of the urn in his churchyard. "You can't do that here!" he yelled across at me. I couldn't help it. I got a fit of the giggles. Oliver and his inappropriate humour had struck again.

I went through the gate and nonchalantly wandered up to the tree on the green and emptied the urn out there. There may or may not have been dog poo at the base of the tree too, but I wasn't looking too closely, I was giggling too hard.

I strutted back to the car park, muttering, "Excellent start to the day, Oliver, just bloody excellent. What next, eh?" and set off to meet the skipper and his wife at the marina. I'd invited the others to join us at a little pier, but I wanted a chance to settle in beforehand. They were a lovely couple who put me at ease straight away.

As we approached the jetty in the boat, I saw only three figures approaching, and the knot in my stomach relaxed. It would be just us, the ones I felt safe with. By this time, John was already having difficulties with his mobility and getting him onto the boat was no small feat, but he was delighted to be on a proper sailboat and with us for the occasion.

We sailed into the channel and, after a little while, the skipper indicated that this was the place where we should do it. I looked at the others and asked if anybody wanted to say anything. No one spoke. I said that I felt I'd pretty much said everything I wanted to say and they agreed, and I said, "Well we can't really just lob him over the side and say *Ciao*, can we?" The response I heard was, "Why not? He'd probably quite like that." So that's what we did.

Oliver and Wiggles, in their biodegradable urn, were merrily lobbed over the side into the water. We all yelled, "Ciao!" and watched the top of the urn bob away.

None of us had discussed it beforehand, but we all came with flowers, and now we scattered them on the water too. It would have made a stunning photo if any of us had been suitably equipped. The bobbing urn top, the flowers, the ripples of the water. One of us said, "I almost wish I'd brought a camera," and there was a feeling of relief that none of us were made to feel awkward about photos being taken.

It was stunning and peaceful, with a view that wouldn't have been out of place on the wall of a yoga studio or meditation room.

There was a sound at the other end of the boat and a little head popped out of the water to say hello.

"Oh, you're in luck today," our skipper said. "That seal doesn't come out for just anybody," and there was collective joy as we acknowledged its presence.

At that point, I felt my choices had been vindicated, for that was my sign that Oliver approved.

As we sailed along, I heard a familiar noise and looked up to the sky. There, above us, were three vintage military aircraft playing in the sky, as if practicing for an air show. They seemed to circle the boat over and over. I smiled. He really liked his send off. I had done well.

But he wasn't done yet, because after the seal and the old aircraft came the murmuration of birds. Thousands of birds dancing in formation in the sky. If I'd never believed in signs, I'd have been hard-pressed not to see that day and its moments of beauty and wonder as anything else.

I finished the day with my best friend, eating burgers while watching the sunset on Portsdown Hill. It was a place I'd been to with Oliver when he was trying to gauge how high or low maintenance I really was. It was the perfect end to a day that I'd been dreading, which had turned out to be a life-affirming experience.

There's another part of the ashes story that came before this.

The Urn

As I said, I had been in possession of Oliver's ashes for some time. In fact, I'd had them since Tilly's christening, because I had wanted him to be there. Ever since, he had sat in his big plastic urn by the pine dresser.

When Wiggles died, he was also cremated and Colin and Melissa brought him to me in his own little urn. I had rather optimistically assumed that combining the two would be easy. I had not factored the weight of Oliver's urn and how difficult it would be to both hold it and the lightweight carboard urn at the same time so that I could tip the contents of the one into the other. I had not factored in the consistency of Oliver's ashes being part dust, part sand sized particles and some gritty bits more like rock salt. I had not anticipated the cloud of dust that would fly up into my face and around the room as I poured some of the grit from the big plastic urn into the cardboard one.

I started to giggle. Then I felt terrible for giggling about the fact that I now had bits of Oliver all over me and all through my hair and that I would have to wash him off and down the drain.

Once I had combined the two, I followed the instructions about gluing on the lid. There was a sachet of PVA glue that you had to spread around the lip of the urn and then quickly put the lid on and close it up to seal it. If you've ever had to open a sachet of ketchup you may be able to imagine my failed attempts with the sachet of PVA glue. I tried to tear it, then used scissors and it went all over my hands and the urn.

I managed to get the lid on and felt as if I'd achieved something important and tricky. Then I surveyed the amount of Oliver and Tigger dust all over the table, the floor, my clothes and Tilly's high chair, which I had forgotten to move out of the way. I brushed the hair out of my face, forgetting that I had PVA glue on my hand, and wondered how best to clear up and if it was right to use the vacuum cleaner.

Using my hands, I tried to sweep the dust off the table, creating yet another dust cloud.

It was time to get the vacuum cleaner. On the way past a mirror, I caught a glimpse of myself. Oh, my days. Between the dust showers and the battle with the PVA I looked like Mary from *There's Something About Mary* when she puts the not-hair-gel in her hair.

The giggles came back, until I was crying with laughter. I had to share this moment with someone, but who on earth could I phone about this, the single most inappropriately hilarious moment in my known world? I called the company I'd bought the urn from. I could hardly speak because I was laughing so hard. I probably sounded like I was crying hysterically, and the lady was so sweet. But then I was clearly laughing and I got the words out and then she was laughing too. "I'm so sorry," I said, "But I just had to share this with someone who would know what I was talking about." She thanked me for brightening up her entire day.

Then I laughed all the way through my shower and thorough hair washing. And I felt grateful to the cheeky monkey with the inappropriate humour who had sent me this mirth to get me through another stage of the process. Because I really, really do believe that it was him and nobody's ever going to convince me otherwise.

The Stump

At Easter in 2011, when I was pregnant, Oliver and I spent a long weekend with my parents. At the top of their garden there was a huge tree stump that Dad hadn't yet broken up for firewood. Oliver took quite a shine to it and there are photos of us in our pyjamas, hugging by that tree stump.

When I bought my house and my parents encouraged me to start thinking about what to do with the garden, pretty much the only thing I was definite about was that I wanted that tree stump. My father indulged me and duly brought it over and put it in the place I had decided it should sit while we figured out what to do with it. It sat in the same spot for five years. I mowed around it and knocked the odd toadstool off to prevent the dogs from eating them, but I never saw the garden as a finished space.

Gardens and their creation had never really been my thing. I enjoyed the gardens that other people had visualised and created, but it wasn't really in my skill set. So, the stump just sat there. In early summer last year, it was partially covered in forget-me-nots. They had self-seeded and flowered for his birthday, in the stump. That stump is exactly where it should be.

They don't really leave until they are ready to.

The signs are there for you to see, hear and feel. You just need to be open to them.

Signs and Me

When you are ready, take out your journal.

Some things may come back to you in a rush, but others will take time. Leave some extra space so that you can come back and add to this bit.

1. Have you experienced any signs? If so, what are they?

2. What emotions have they brought to the surface?

3. How have they helped you through the grieving process?

Part Three

Letting Go

Seven whole years
from then to now
slow quick slow quick
the earth turned 'round.

Forty-eight days
you're longer gone
than I knew you.
It hit me hard.

Last night crying
silent tears, mixed
with ugly sobs.
My body hurts,

Woke up to see
the rain had cleared,
sun was shining,
a new day dawns.

Just another
day without you
slow quick slow quick
the earth turns 'round.

1.11.18

Secrets and Lies

"I never claimed to be a paragon of virtue"
Oliver Lund

Oliver made a point of telling me that he didn't want to be remembered as anything other than who and what he was. When I look back with the benefit of hindsight, he had said as much to me in different ways from that first time we met, at the job interview. It was like no job interview I'd ever been to. As part of the banter, he was open with me about having been in trouble with the police for his youthful speeding habit.

He had warned me that he was 'famous' in his little seaside village, then grinned and giggled and said, "Well, maybe *notorious* is a better way of putting it," before guffawing at the notion that anybody might mistake him for a celebrity.

Writing that has just made me laugh, as I remember him recounting the time when he was chatting to a lovely couple on the beach. Afterwards, someone asked him, "What's she like then?!" He hadn't realised that he'd been obliviously chatting to Emma Bunton of the Spice Girls.

The next time I saw him was in the lounge bar on the floor below his office, where he introduced me to his boss and the rest of his team. We talked over our soft drinks. Everyone else had hit the bar because it was between Christmas and New Year and the office had just closed for a long New Year's weekend. He told me he didn't drink. There was a catch in his voice, like he wanted to say more but was struggling with whether he should or not. "Is there a reason for that, then?" I asked and he said, "Yes, I'm a recovering alcoholic." He said it in a nervous way that made me think he was expecting me to get up, throw my lemonade in his face and strop off into the sunset.

Of course, I didn't do that. I said something that I hoped was reassuring. I spoke to him again over that weekend, while out partying. I won't pretend that I was the most thoughtful twentysomething while drunk, but I improved over time.

As I got to know him, I gradually uncovered layers of his life and I was left in no doubt as to why he was notorious.

He was, as my mother would put it, a cheeky monkey.

The Other Women

There was his history with his ex. They had worked together and she was old enough to be his mother. He had set his cap at her feet and, from what I was told, pretty much wore down her resistance until they were living together.

She lived in this incredible house made of railway carriages, set one row back from the beach. When the houses between her place and the beach came up for sale, she begged him not to buy them. So, he bought them. She begged him not to live there, under her nose, with other women. So, he did that too.

And every time it went wrong, he'd go back to her for comfort.

I met her once while he still lived in the beach house and I could see that having her on side would be essential for anyone wanting to make a life with Oliver. Defining their relationship was beyond me. He occasionally referred to her as his ex, but mostly he called her by her name. This was probably because when he said, "My ex", I'd say, "Which one?" (there were a few of them).

Their bond was incredibly strong. I met her again when he was moving out of that house. We laughed at the childish love letters scattered all over the house, we cooed over ancient passport photos of Oliver as a very young man and teased each other over the fact that we were packing his stuff while he was faffing about making cups of tea and smoking, and his girlfriend was nowhere to be seen.

That's right, at that point, there was a girlfriend.

I'd actually worked out quite quickly that Oliver operated something of a harem. If I'd been a different version of myself than the 27-year-old who fell for him hook, line and sinker, it might have put me off. In a strange way, it actually made him more appealing.

The relationship I'd been in before I met Oliver was extremely unhealthy and, having felt smothered and then stalked by that man, this was a refreshing change.

Oliver was somebody who wouldn't let me go, but also wouldn't ever say things like, "I can't wait to get you pregnant, because then you can never leave me."

That's not to say that Oliver didn't talk about having babies. He would throw it into the conversation all the time. Sometimes it would be, "You do know, don't you, that I will have my way and you will rent out all the rooms in your house and come live with me and have my babies?" At other times, it would be, "It wouldn't be the worst idea in the world if we had a baby, would it?"

I figured it was all just banter and I'd volley back with some humorous comment about how having a kid with him would be taking on the parenting of two at once, or how babies shouldn't be brought into the world just to help overgrown children get their shit together.

By the time we made our baby, about six years after we first met, we no longer said those flippant things. He knew I wanted a baby and he knew I wanted that baby to be his.

We both knew making a baby wouldn't fix him, but it might fix a piece of me.

There was no great fairy-tale romance for us, but there was love and laughter and an acknowledged air of 'to the death' about our relationship. For at least the first five years, I was no more capable of a grown-up committed relationship than he was. We shared a string of disconnected moments, spent hundreds of hours on the phone to each other, having fractured conversations as we drove in and out of signal, made love like there was no tomorrow, did things in our cars that I won't confess to in writing, walked on beaches, went on random adventures with our dogs, painted his bathroom, danced in a private disco, played in his boat and went out in his supercars.

He had this friend up the beach who could have been a retired builder or a retired mobster. I prefer to think of him as the latter, because he used to tease me about getting a pole put into his living room so I could come and dance for him. I'd laugh and remind him that podium dancing and pole dancing are different, and maybe he was mixing me up with one of the others. The first time I said that, he spat his drink all over the place. I don't think any of Oliver's other girlfriends acknowledged that there were other women. Maybe they didn't know, maybe they didn't care.

I was wearing a top that day from the 2003 Robbie Williams concert at Knebworth and it had 03 on the chest. "See," I said, laughing and pointing at it, "I'm number three." He laughed and said, "You'd be my number one darlin', but Olly's a law unto himself."

There was a bizarrely funny conversation that Oliver and I had while I was pregnant. He was trawling his memory banks to find a girlfriend he hadn't cheated on. He assured me there was one. I asked him who and he told me her name. I simply laughed and told him he was mistaken. He looked confused, as if he was trying to do mental arithmetic. Then he looked at me and said, "Who did I cheat on her with, then? It wasn't *X* because that was after…" I reminded him that he'd invited me down to his place for a night of fun and I'd tripped over the shoes the other girl had left on the floor at the end of his bed.

I'm also under no illusion that he was faithful while I was pregnant. I refused to give up work before I qualified for maternity pay, so he had an awful lot of time on his hands. He didn't like being alone and couldn't bear silence. I think his demons haunted him so constantly by then that if he didn't have at least one thing to distract him, they consumed him.

Nothing about our set-up was ideal. But it was ours.

We made our own little dysfunctional unit. We both knew it was the best either of us could make it at that point in time.

During my pregnancy, I also spent countless hours preparing court documents, dealing with the police, going to see solicitors and attending court dates with him. Some of this was because he was desperate to see his firstborn, and some was because of his downward spiral. Moments of being gloriously happy about the new person I was growing in my belly were often squashed by having to discuss his exes and the business contacts who had screwed him over.

Fairy Tales?

Did I wish it was more of a fairy tale? Sometimes.

But then I would remember that, in order to have a fairy tale romance, I'd have needed to be an incredibly sheltered teenage girl and he'd have needed to be a prince with big shoulders, shapely calves and no baggage.

Oh, how I'd laugh at that notion.

I know the people who loved me wanted him to be more like a prince, wanted him to pledge his undying devotion and sweep me off my feet. Some of them even told me so. And I love them for that. However, the big 'but' is that they forget I wasn't baggage-free either. And, when the fairy-tale prince did try to sweep me off my feet, I couldn't handle the pedestal he put me on, so I destroyed it (sorry G).

People with great self-esteem probably don't get involved with damaged people who are not actively working to getting better. If they do, they either get unwell too or they leave.

He didn't want our daughter to grow up thinking he was a saint, and he didn't want his other daughter growing up thinking he was a monster.

Revelations

Over the past few years, I have gradually revealed to Tilly, a little at a time, the reality of the Daddie she never knew. She knows that he was "a silly billy" who crashed into things a lot. She knows that he and I didn't have a meet, fall in love, get married, live happily ever after until he died relationship. I dropped in that there had been other girlfriends for Daddie and other boyfriends for me and I let that sit for a few months. Then, last summer, I told her about her half-sister.

It was a secret I'd been wrestling with for a long time. But I'm happy I have done the best I can to present my little girl with bits of information in digestible chunks and in age-appropriate ways.

As an only child, Tilly has, at various times, either longed for a sibling or been grateful to not have to share me. When she was little and saw her friends getting new little brothers and sisters, she would ask me when she was getting hers, as if we could go to Tesco and choose one. I would then explain that babies are made by two people and I didn't have another person to make a baby with.

I quietly hoped that I might meet somebody wonderful who had a little girl of a similar age, so they could each get the part-time sibling they wanted. But it was not to be.

Then Oliver's other daughter got in touch with Melissa and putting off the chat with Tilly for much longer looked like it might create much bigger problems down the line. It would, after all, be beyond awful for Tilly to hear about this half-sister from somebody else.

I looked at our calendar and decided that the fairest time to tell her would be at the start of the summer holidays. That would give her several weeks to digest and process this new information and ask questions before she went back to school. We were also due to spend a week at Colin and Melissa's and they were more than happy to answer any of Tilly's questions.

We went for a walk to a place that we'd been to before, but which wasn't one of our regular walks. I wanted somewhere with the comfort of familiarity, but not a favourite place that would be tinged with bad memories if it all went horribly wrong. We walked with the dogs and left the path that we normally took to follow a different track.

"Do you remember I said that Daddie had other girlfriends and I had other boyfriends?"

"Yes?"

Deep breath. "Well, the thing is, Daddie had one in particular that he was on and off with for a long time, like he was with me. But they seemed to bring out the worst in each other and couldn't be friends."

"Okay."

"And, a few years before Daddie and I made you, he made a baby with her."

"Okay."

"And I feel that you are old enough and grown up enough to know about her now."

"Okay."

"Would you like to know about her?"

"Okay."

So, I told her what little I knew and we carried on walking until I suggested we turn back.

I had rehearsed these bits in advance so that I could detach my feelings about the child's mother and the legal battle she had fought over Oliver's estate. Her child is innocent, and Oliver loved her very much. I focussed on the nice things that Melissa had said about her.

That was over a year ago and the only thing Tilly asked was whether the other girl knew about her. I told her yes, I thought she did.

It's a lot to take in when you're seven years old. There is no way to know if they will have a relationship in the future, but the secret is out and now Tilly can choose whether she wants to do anything with it.

As she grows up, we will no doubt have difficult conversations about her Grannie's death and about alcohol and drugs. But she has more than enough to cope with right now.

The Temptation to Deify or Demonise

When somebody dies, particularly when they die suddenly, there is often a temptation to make them two dimensional, so that we see only their light or dark side.

Princess Diana is a good example. In the months leading up to her sudden and untimely death, the British media had run countless stories that were critical of her personal life and of her attempts to continue using her profile to do good. Her death was on the cover of every newspaper in the UK and many other countries within hours of its occurrence.

Suddenly, the same papers that had made millions from snide commentary about her every move now cashed in on hero worship.

It was bizarre.

Prime Minister Tony Blair called her the People's Princess. Flowers and teddy bears and candles and placards and every tribute imaginable were left outside the palace gates.

She was remembered with almost saintly reverence by the same people who had judged her so harshly only days earlier.

Part of this press U-turn may have been because the accident probably wouldn't have happened if her car hadn't been chased by paparazzi photographers. Maybe there were some guilty consciences at the tabloids, or maybe the hero worship was just a way to sell more papers.

Maybe the general public really had always loved her, or maybe they also felt guilty for having judged this 36-year-old woman so harshly.

In any event, the media and the general mood of the time worked together to deify Princess Diana.

Paparazzi photographers were widely blamed. The tabloid newspapers were also blamed for their role in driving demand for the photographs. What few people were willing to accept, however, was that the demand for the photos was every bit as driven by the *individuals* who bought the newspapers.

Demonising the paparazzi and the tabloids shifted blame and guilt away from ourselves.

A similar process can happen when a person dies prematurely or ends their own life, particularly if they can be seen to have been driven by external pressures.

Those left behind may choose to focus entirely on the good they saw in the person, and may choose to focus the blame entirely on a third party or parties.

When Oliver died, there was a strong feeling, often vocalised within his family, that he was dead because of the behaviour of two particular individuals.

I will certainly not defend the way they behaved towards him. I do, however, think it's too simplistic to focus only on their input, even if it is more comfortable to do so.

When Erica died, I blamed John. I still believe that if he'd died first, or agreed to move into a residential facility, she would have been able to live the simple life she craved. She'd probably still be alive. But that is my perspective based entirely on my observations of them and my conversations with her. She may also have been depressed about other things, but everything I saw and heard pointed in that single direction.

I have heard that she wasn't the most welcoming stepmother when the twins were younger, but I never experienced her as anything other than a true friend and a doting grandmother to my daughter. My perspective of her as a person and of the circumstances of her death are, therefore, quite two dimensional.

My paternal grandfather was one of my favourite people. I wrote a eulogy for his funeral. When I read it to my dad, he looked confused. The man I described was so unlike the man my father had grown up with.

What can seem to be the absolute truth to one person may sound ridiculous to somebody else who knew them in a different way. That is the great paradox of perspective.

My relationship with Colin and Melissa has allowed me to remember Oliver as he truly was, the way he showed up to the people he felt safest with. It has made it so much easier to reveal him as a real person to his daughter. She hears about him from them as much as she hears about him from me.

Confession time. I absolutely blame him for things that he is not here to defend himself over. It is a running family joke. When Tilly displays stubbornness, I say she gets it from her father. When she is cheeky, I say she gets it from her father. She gets these things in equal measure from both of us, but I like to mention him whenever I feel like it and I like to think it's good for her to know she is not just a product of me.

When we choose how to remember somebody, it can be helpful to focus on the good bits to begin with. A vital part of this process, however, is also acknowledging the rest.

My Secrets, My Lies and My Truth

When you are ready, take out your journal.

1. Which parts of my story do I keep secret?

2. Why do I feel that I should keep them secret?

3. What are the lies I tell about my story?

    a. What are the lies I tell others?

    b. What are the lies I tell myself?

4. What am I hiding from behind these secrets and lies?

5. Why am I afraid?

6. What is my truth?

Clearing the Wreckage

The stuff.

So much stuff.

When I talk about clearing the wreckage, there is so much more to it than the physical stuff. But it is the physical stuff that is visible. You can actually see that you are making progress through the changes in the physical stuff, even on those days when you don't feel as if you've made any progress at all.

The stuff can take many, many forms.

I wore his clothes in that period between clearing out his house and going to the States to visit my bestie. I wore the things I had bought him for his last Christmas – the stripy dressing gown and the rugby tops that we finally agreed on after spending ages looking for just the right thing. I wore his jeans. We had spent hours in TK

Maxx as he tried on pairs of jeans until he found the pair he liked. I wore his aftershave.

It all made me feel closer to him.

It was also part of my identity crisis. Having just had a baby, my body didn't spring back into its pre-pregnancy shape overnight. I didn't want to carry on wearing my maternity clothes. And the clothes in my wardrobe didn't fit. I didn't need the smart work clothes that I could fit into, because that was no longer my world or my life. Who in their right mind would wear dry-clean only clothes around a baby?

His clothes fitted me, and I felt close to him. It felt right to cuddle our baby while wearing his clothes, as it was the closest that I could get to being him, for her. The closest she would ever get to being held in the loving embrace of her father.

I knew that I was on dangerous ground though. I knew it wasn't healthy. I didn't want to *be* him. I just didn't want our daughter to never know him.

Hunting for ways to fill the gaps that he left was a constant whirring in the background of my mind. Neither of us wanted her to experience the sad or bad bits – the father who didn't trust his body not to drop her, the man tortured and often crippled by relentless pain throughout his nervous system, the intensity of his frustration and loathing for those who had wronged him.

But there was so much more to him than that. I wanted her to have known those bits. I wanted her to have known his laugh, to have known the creases by the sides of his eyes when he was up to mischief, to have known the all-healing envelopment of his hugs. I wanted her to have letters filled with wisdom to open on her special birthdays, and videos to watch of them playing together when she was older. I wanted *her* to have so many memories of him that she simply would never have.

So, I held on to my memories of him, and anybody else's memories that were on offer. That way, I had something to share with her when she was old enough to see and feel those gaps.

I didn't want to let go of even a single piece of paper that he'd scribbled on. I wanted to be able to share these things with our daughter, who never knew him, so that she could feel closer to him. I wanted those bits of stuff to fill all of the gaps in her life because I couldn't see how else to protect her from the void inside *me*.

And so, I kept things.

The house we rented had a garage, and the garage was filled with his furniture, and with boxes. There was the huge antique pine tallboy, huge oak chest of drawers, three kitchen tables, each with at least four chairs, a rubber dinghy and several sets of oars, his coat collection with at least three mouldy-looking waxed jackets. Every drawer was filled with random bits of his paraphernalia. There were more boxes in the house. Legal paperwork going back several years, old business cards he'd collected, a huge cutlery collection of indeterminate origin, artwork that may or may not have had any intrinsic value, and his clothes.

His Clothes

For a man who, for the most part, wore a dressing gown or, at best, jeans and a t-shirt, Oliver had an impressive collection of shirts. I had lovingly washed and ironed all of them when he came to stay with me in London. I'd even cleared out an entire wardrobe of my things so that his shirts could hang nicely. He'd been overcome when he saw them, and surprised that anybody would care enough about him to wash and iron the shirts and do the buttons up in such a way that he could put them on over his head, leaving him with only one button to struggle with.

I'd watched him start to take care of his appearance again now that he had his shirts to wear. Those shirts reminded him of his life before, the life where people listened to him and agreed that, while he was a massive pain in the arse at times, he was full of great ideas.

His shirts reminded him of feeling confident and of being

visible. He held himself differently when he wore a clean, ironed shirt. He showered every day and even shaved occasionally. The shirts were important. The shirts held good memories for him then and they retain good memories for me, even now.

The shirts have been washed and ironed again since he died. They hung in a wardrobe again for a while, but I knew I never wanted anybody else to wear them. His favourite short-sleeved rugby top had gone astray by the time I cleared the house, and he was cremated in the guernsey my parents bought him that last Christmas. The shirts stayed and have a special destiny.

I had much less attachment to his t-shirts and there were several pairs of shorts and slip-on summer shoes to which I felt no connection. But I couldn't bear the prospect of going into town and seeing somebody else walking around in his clothes, and neither of us were fans of throwing things out that could have utility value for somebody else. I held onto them for another year or so, until the typhoon hit the Philippines. There was a collection at the local church. It was perfect. People far away who genuinely needed these clothes.

I filled the car boot and, with shaking hands, handed them over. It was the first piece of letting go I had done in over a year. I drove home and cried, but I knew they were tears of relief rather than sadness. I had found a 'right' way to let go of something.

A way had presented itself to me that allowed me to let go of *things* that didn't mean I was throwing *him* away. It was a way that honoured his beliefs about helping people who really need help, and it fulfilled my need to not be confronted by them again, once they had been let go.

It helped me to then let go of things such as the dishwasher and to agree to having the excess furniture sold at auction when it was time for me to move house. I could get rid of the things I had no strong emotional attachment to. It was no longer 'keep everything', but it was still 'keep almost everything'.

Within weeks of the third anniversary of Oliver's death, Tilly and I moved into our new home. I made a conscious decision to first put up the pictures that *I* loved, rather than leading with his. You see, in the rental house in which he had never set foot, his artwork had taken pride of place while mine was on the floor behind the sofa. That house had, in some ways, been like a shrine. There were framed photos of him everywhere and the dining room was entirely dominated by the pine dresser.

The Dresser

Most girls and women apparently get excited about engagement rings. I wanted to be excited, but I was struggling. He still talked about death so much that I hesitated. I can now look at my uncertainty at that time with the benefit of hindsight. I think that some part of me thought that if we were married it would be worse, more painful, when he died than if we weren't married.

Putting time and energy into choosing rings was, therefore, encouraging swifter and deeper pain at his loss. Also, he kept looking at hideously over-the-top rings online, and I didn't want him to choose something that I'd never want to wear!

What I could get excited about, however, was a pine dresser.

The Sunday mornings of my childhood had been spent watching shows like *The Waltons* and, in my mind, a big pine dresser was more strongly associated with marital harmony than any diamond. At the same time that we were choosing a rental house near my parents to move into, their neighbours were downsizing and they had put their beautiful dresser up for sale. He saw my eyes light up and bought it for me.

That dresser represented our commitment to each other far more than any ring ever could.

It ended up in storage while Tilly and I lived with my parents. The only part of my life with Oliver that it featured in was the day he bought it.

When it was time to move out into a rental house, I needed a wall big enough to stand it against. The fact that it was too big for our rental house was by the by. It so dominated the dining room of that house that I could only fit a tiny table in with it, and the proper sized tables all went into the garage.

When I started to look for a place to buy with what was left of his estate, having a house that accommodated the dresser was non-negotiable. I converted the garage of our new home into a kitchen so that the dresser had a home.

Yes, really. The dresser meant that much to me.

The dresser also completely overwhelmed the space in our new house and meant we ended up with stuff dumped all over it and on the floor in front of it, because the furniture we had and the space we had didn't really work. For three years, the dresser remained more important than the usability of the space.

The dresser represented our commitment, and it represented him understanding my outlook. It represented the moment when he saw that my otherness from all of his previous and other women was very real. I was never with him for his fast cars and I didn't care about diamonds. The dresser was so much more than a big lump of wood.

It certainly was a big lump of wood. It got in the way and it dominated the ground floor of our house and it was so covered in stuff that it looked like crap, and that crap was reflected in the big mirror that was supposed to make the room look bigger. My rational mind could see that the dresser was *in my way*.

I sat with that thought, once it had materialised in my rational mind.

I started to imagine what else could change if the dresser was no longer there. I started to visualise alternative furniture layouts, where we could move the table out of the living room and make a dining area in the kitchen, and how that would change the way we ate together. I started to visualise how differently the sofas could be arranged and how much bigger the living room would look without the table and chairs. I started to visualise how different the reflection in the big mirror would be if there was a white wall instead of a tall heavily-laden dresser.

I started to want the alternative vision more than the dresser.

Then I sat with my attachment and my feelings.

Did keeping the dresser have any impact on whether or not Oliver had loved me? No.

Did keeping the dresser have any impact on whether I had loved him, or how much? No.

Was keeping the dresser of any benefit to our daughter? No.

So, why the fuck was I keeping the dresser?

I emptied it out, cleaned it up, took photos and listed it on eBay. The lady who bought it really wanted it, and I knew that she would love it the way it deserved to be loved. I helped the man who came to pick it up to get it out of the house. I closed the door behind him, got stuck into cleaning the floor and felt a huge sense of lightness.

This again had been, for me, the right way and the right time for letting go.

His Suits

It took me the best part of another year to feel ready to say goodbye to his suits.

Oliver was passionate about helping homeless people get back on their feet. I think he found London a bit spiritually overwhelming because he saw himself in so many of the homeless men on its streets. Sometimes he could do what Londoners do, and walk by obliviously, but other times, he could not. When he was feeling particularly shaky in his AA recovery, he would identify so closely with those cold and dirty men lying on cardboard with despair or glassiness in their eyes, that he wept.

His desire to be useful beyond the boundaries of his natural life was strong. He had been keen to donate his body to medical research, because he felt it might be useful in studying the long-term impact of alcoholism, pain medication and orthopaedic reconstruction.

He only changed his mind when he was informed that, at some point in the future, I would be contacted to ask if I wanted what was left of him. I remain grateful that he chose cremation, so that the closure and the timelines associated with it were not in somebody else's hands.

I had asked around if there was such a thing as a repository for suits to help homeless or struggling men prepare for job interviews. The same name kept coming up – Suited & Booted in London. It took me months, if not a year, to make the call and speak to them. It took me several more months to wrap up his high street and designer label suits.

I laid them all out on the bed in the spare room. All but one. I smelled them. I triple checked the pockets. I folded, refolded and then rolled them. I thanked them for making him feel good when he had worn them. I put them into the big bag, ready for posting.

Then, I took a deep breath and reached back into the wardrobe. I touched the sleeve of his favourite suit, the one he'd been wearing when we met. For a moment, I was immediately transported to that ridiculous excuse for a job interview, with Wiggles lying on my feet.

And then I wasn't grinning any more. I was back in the present day and he was gone and I was holding the sleeve of a suit I'd never want to see anybody else wear. I dried my eyes, held the suit close like I was hugging him goodbye and added it to the bag.

There were shoes too, shoes we had bought together and I knew had only been worn a handful of times. Part of me said I should try to sell them, but I just couldn't bring myself to do that. So, I wrapped them and put them in the big bag too. And then, I waited another couple of weeks to make sure, before sending them on their way.

It would be a lie to say that they left my mind when I walked away from the courier point. I felt a weight leave my shoulders, but they were still on my mind. Had I chosen the right place? Would they definitely be doing what he would have wanted? But then, I received an email. The lady who ran the charity knew the origin of the suits, and she knew that it had been a hugely emotionally-driven donation. She had taken the time to make sure that I knew they had been received.

Then there was the sign. A "Well done, it's exactly what I wanted" sign from Oliver. Somebody entirely unconnected to Oliver or to me shared a video on Facebook about the lady who ran the charity and the people she helped. I knew, without a doubt, that this was another right way of letting go, while entirely honouring him.

The suits took me seven years. I still have the shirts.

The Table

In the eighth year, I let go of more. I have found it easier over time to see his things simply as things.

If they do not serve our needs, they should go and serve somebody else's. I am writing this chapter in my home office, at a desk my father gave me when he reorganised his work space. For the first four and a half years that I lived in this house, my home office largely served as a dumping ground. I would sporadically clear it out, and then watch it refill.

I struggled to understand why it was so hard to sit down and focus when I was in the office. Yes, there is a lot of stuff in this room. It houses my sewing, art and craft materials, as well as my stationery addiction and a fair number of books.

But there was more to it than that. I felt blocked by something, something that made me not want to be in here. It took me a long time to realise that the table I had set up as my erstwhile desk had been Oliver's kitchen table.

When we were clearing his house, I had insisted on keeping it. I wanted Tilly to eat her breakfast at the table where her father had eaten his breakfast, even if they never did it together. I had a romanticised notion. I don't know if he regularly sat down to eat breakfast at a table. Oliver was the king of eating on the sofa.

My mind then wandered to asking myself the painful questions of what else had he used the table for, and who had he been with? Once my mind had gone to that place, the table had to go.

My friend Zoe, a no-nonsense decluttering legend who had been itching to get into my house and start clearing it for me, was delighted to help. The table left the house, and I started to feel inspired again. It is strange and obvious all at the same time how powerful our emotional connections to the things in our lives can be.

Getting rid of somebody's stuff doesn't mean you're throwing the person away. It just means you're no longer holding on to their stuff simply because it was theirs. If it's not useful or intrinsically beautiful in a way that you can't bear not to have it, let go of it. Embrace your own identity and your own tastes.

Having your person in your heart negates the need to have them all over your home.

Me and The Stuff
Get out your journal.

1. Make a list of the stuff you have inherited – furniture, clothing, books, boxes, all of it.

2. Ask yourself why you still have it.

   a. Is it useful in your life?

   b. Do you inherently like/love it?

   c. Do you need it because of legal proceedings?

   The things for which you can answer truthfully "yes" to

a, b and c, above, you can move past right now. You may wish to come back and do the Marie Kondo "Do they spark joy?" test in the future, but let's look at the other stuff first.

    d. Do you feel ready to let it go, but lack the motivation to do so?

        i. Selling things on platforms such as eBay can be great if they have inherent value and you have the time to devote to the listing, packaging and posting processes. Be ruthless when you ask yourself if an item is *worth* selling? And do you really have the time to do it?

            1. If your answer is yes, get on with it.

            2. If your answer is no, you can offer it to friends or donate it to charity.

        ii. Do you have boxes or bags of stuff ready to go to the charity shop, or the dump, but they never seem to leave the house? Ask for help. Family, friends and neighbours have all helped me to get stuff out of my house. If you have furniture to donate, some charities will come and collect. If you have lots of stuff to go to the dump, the council may be willing to collect large items such as furniture or white goods.

    e. Do you feel overwhelmed and unsure where to even start?

        i. Start small. Pick a drawer or a box, and start there. Just do that one drawer or that one box until you have finished sorting it. Then do another one. And so on.

ii. Get help. Whether it's a friend, a family member or a professional declutterer, getting help makes asking the "Keep? Sell? Donate? Bin?" questions much easier.

3. What does this stuff add to your life?

4. What does this stuff prevent you from being in your life?

5. What does the stuff represent for you?

6. What does letting go of this stuff represent for you?

7. What might a 'right way' of letting go of stuff look like for you?

Making Space

So, if I've rid myself of the excess stuff, why am I talking about making space? Haven't I already made space by clearing out my home?

I'm not talking about that kind of space.

This is about making space in your heart.

Don't worry, the stuff that you need to declutter from your heart isn't love. We all have an infinite capacity for love.

It's like when people have a second child and, up until the moment they connect with that second child, they fear that they can't possibly love it as much as the first one. But then they do and it's all okay.

I only have one child so, from my own experience, I know this from my deep and enduring devotion to the great canine companions who have been such a huge part of my heart and life.

When Pip died, I didn't think I'd ever love anyone or anything that much again. When Mackie, my confidante and physical therapist through my twenties, died, I had the exact same sensation. Now I have George and I know that I will one day face her loss and it will devastate me all over again. I know that she will not be my last dog, because the love I have for her will need to go somewhere else.

You can love and lose and love again.

The love is all good.

The love that you can feel beyond the recovery from loss is just as big, if not bigger than the love you felt before. This love does not have to be of the romantic kind in order for you to tap into the great well of infinite happiness. You can be perfectly happy without a life partner if you have mastered being happy with yourself. I know I can be perfectly happy without a man. I have friends who have also chosen to be the captains of their own ships.

I also know that, until I had been through this process of decluttering my heart, I was missing out on much deeper friendships with some phenomenal women. That is why I feel it is essential to include this here.

What we need to declutter from our hearts are our walls.

The walls are made from fear. Some fears are so big and deep that they are like solid bricks. Some are smaller but sticky, forming the mortar between the bricks. These are solid and they obscure opportunities from our vision. Others are like translucent glass, where you can see enough to know that there is something on the other side, but you can't tell what it is. And then there are the fears that are like locked windows. You can see what's on the other side, but you can't touch it, even if you want to.

Over the years, I have heard many acronyms for fear that have appealed to me. Oliver's favourite was Fuck Everything And Run. My friend Sam's is False Evidence Appearing Real and mine is Face Everything And Recover.

Fear is part of the primitive make-up of our brains. We have a section of the brain that holds our fight or flight instincts and it works based on messages, or maybe flag waving, within the subconscious. When you make a negative association with something, that message gets sent to that layer of the brain, so that when you see that thing again you want to get away from it.

It's a very useful way for us to learn not to touch fire with the naked hand, which is helpful for our survival. It can also be a highly effective way of sabotaging our growth and development.

When you think about making space in your heart and letting someone else in, that primitive layer of your brain may go into a little frenzy of activity. Its entire purpose is to protect you. What it chooses to protect you from varies from one person to the next but, at its root, it is protecting you from pain.

For some of us, it may be the fear of losing another loved one and having to go through the grief process all over again. "Will they die on me too?" is as valid for a best friend as it is for a romantic partner.

If one of my best friends died, would I allow someone else to become that important to me again, in the knowledge that they might also leave me behind?

Yes. I would.

I know this, because I have let best friends go before and, while it hurt each and every time, I survived and it made space for a better friendship to grow in its place.

Real enduring friendship is built on loyalty and shared experience. None of us is perfect, but there must be a balance in any lasting relationship where the responsibility for supporting the other person is shared. This balance is what enables both partners to keep showing up for each other, as well as themselves, and finding forgiveness when it is needed.

In romantic relationships, that balance is even more essential. The fear may show itself in very obvious ways, or it may be more subtle.

My fears about letting somebody else in largely stem from what I have experienced in my life. I can add a few extra bits from what those around me have experienced, but mostly my fears are about avoiding the repetition of mistakes I have made in the past.

Honesty is required. Brutal honesty.

I speak for myself, but I know I am not alone.

What follows is a catalogue of fears that spilled out of me onto the keyboard with alarming speed. You'll see what I mean about the obvious and the more subtle fears.

My track record of picking people who were damaged is impressive, which wouldn't be so bad if they were trying to heal themselves, but most of them weren't.

What am I missing out on by being by myself?

I feel no great void of loneliness.

I don't miss having somebody beside me when I sleep. In truth, since she became a nocturnal octopus, I don't even like sleeping with my child. I like sleeping with my dog and that's about it.

I don't have time to kill. Ever.

I don't miss having somebody to call to say goodnight.

I don't miss having somebody to talk through my day with, because if I have anything interesting to say I talk to my daughter or a friend.

I have been on my own for so long now that I have my own relationships with my friends' husbands. I don't feel like they struggle to talk to me or wish there was somebody more 'blokey' they could be talking to instead at barbeques or while waiting to pick our kids up from Brownies.

I watch and I listen and from what I see of my friends' relationships, co-parenting is what they share most at this stage of their lives. I have no idea how to do that. I don't know if Tilly would even want me to.

It is very easy to talk myself out of even trying.

What if I let in another person who would drag me down again? What if this time they dragged me all the way under? I have a child now who is entirely dependent on me – I can't afford that kind of mistake.

Could I trust my judgement?

Could I trust and take that leap of faith?

Then there are my experiences of living with other adults.

I've lived with people who are noisy, selfish and lazy. I've even lived with people who won't recycle.

I used to relish the big rows with Oliver, when he'd pack his bag and strop off back to his house for a night, because it meant I could clean my flat and Febreze the living daylights out of it to get rid of the smell of cigarettes.

In my house, the mess is mine and Tilly's. If there are clothes on the floor, they're usually hers, she's nine and we're making progress on using the laundry basket. If there are mugs left around the house, they're mine. Yes, I sometimes mutter FFS under my breath as I take yet another load of toys back up to her room from the living room, but she is my child and I am her mother and I figure this is part of that role.

What if I let someone in who left their stuff all over the house?

What if I let someone in who left massive size 11 shoes in the front hall, or even worse, never took them off and walked through the house wearing them?!

Or what if it was bigger stuff?

What if I let someone in who manipulated me? What if I let someone in who I ended up afraid of?

What if I let someone in who wasn't kind to my little girl?

Can you see how easy it is to build the wall? In a matter of minutes, you can go from breezy and *"Yeah, if I tripped over someone great, I could totally get back into that relationship thing"*, to *"Batten down the hatches, we're under attack!"*

Making space in our hearts to share love again is big and brave.

It's also an investment in our happiness.

So How Do We Do This?

Do you remember Whitney Houston's rendition of *The Greatest Love of All*? I spent countless hours of my childhood pretending I could belt it out with her range. The lyrics emphasised the vital importance of self-love. If you love who you are and lead a life that you take pride in, you will naturally attract people who are also happy in their own skins and capable of being in a relationship with you that is not overwhelming or smothering. Your interest in people who are not on your wavelength will be noticeably reduced.

Your capacity to give and receive love with others is predicated on your capacity for self-love.

Sounds great. But how do I do this?

Let's take a moment to take some deep deliberate breaths.

Breathe in faith, fill your whole body, hold it, and release.

Breathe out fear. All the way out.

And again, breathe in faith, breathe out fear.

Forgiveness

The biggest and most important thing is forgiveness.

Forgive yourself for whatever guilt you are still holding on to.

We are all doing the best we can. Sometimes our best wasn't that great, but it was the best we could offer at the time.

In real life, you don't get do-overs. If you fucked it up the first time, you may be given an opportunity to try again, but you don't start from the same place. Anyone who's ever tried to patch up a relationship will relate to this – you have a fight, you break up, you decide it was a bad decision, you get back together, but you can't un-say what you said in the fight. You can apologise, but those words are still out in the world.

The best you can do is practice forgiveness and do better as you move forward.

If that doesn't feel like enough for you, look for ways to balance out your karma. Do more good things than you might have done before. Get into a habit of complimenting people when you notice they look great, instead of just thinking it in your head – it might change the course of their whole day. Be a proactive positive ripple maker. Go check on your elderly neighbour – you might be the only person they talk to all day. Volunteer for a charity or a good cause. There are so many ways you can help make the world better and make yourself feel better in the process.

Forgive Others

Forgive them for whatever guilt you feel they should or should not be burdened by.

Easier said than done? I know.

Remember when I talked about my history and the incidents in my fledgling years that drove me into the black pit? Trust me, I get it.

With the benefit of hindsight and distance, I can see that *some* of the people who hurt me did so because of their own pain. I can also see that some of them hurt me more than once because I chose to stay in their path rather than learning from the first time and getting out of the way, or because my low self-worth had me believing that their treatment of me was what I deserved.

I have chosen to forgive them, and myself, because we were all doing the best we could with what we had at the time.

That doesn't cover all of them though. I cannot see how anyone could justify some of the things that have been done to me. So, I forgive a different way. I have not chosen to forgive them because

I think *they* deserve it. I have chosen to forgive them because *I* deserve to not carry that anger around inside me.

I have a quote attributed to Buddha (which may or may not have actually come from Buddha, but that's not what's important right now) that sums up this need to forgive others for our own benefit:

"Holding on to anger is like drinking poison and expecting the other person to die."

Another quote that I have found helpful for certain people, but for which I can find no source, is:

"Sometimes the first step to forgiveness is realising the other person is batshit crazy."

> Forgiving someone doesn't mean inviting them
> back into your life, it means letting go of the anger
> and pain you feel.

Whatever perspective you need to take, find a way to forgive.

And, don't worry, karma catches up with all of us eventually. You just need to accept that it won't give you a ringside seat when it does.

Let's take a couple more of those deep breaths.

Breathe in faith, fill up your whole body, hold it, and release.

Breathe out fear, let it all go. And again.

Breathe in faith, breathe out fear.

In letting go of the guilt, you free up so much space.

Unpicking Fears

Now, let's pick apart those fears. One by one, let's look at them and get curious.

Let's start with the obvious, "What if they die on me too?"

Honestly, unless one of you has a serious health condition, or one of you is much older than the other, there's a 50:50 probability that they will die first. Meaning there's also a 50:50 probability that they won't.

In addition, you already have a proven track record of getting through loss.

So, ask yourself the question, "What if?" What are the specific things you think might happen, or the specific things you might feel, if you were to meet someone and they were to die before you?

Then ask yourself how likely that is to happen.

Then ask yourself, "What if it doesn't happen?"

Can you look at those specific fears and rewrite the story?

I'll use one of my big fears as an example. "What if I let somebody in who I end up being afraid of?"

This goes back to the boyfriend who was smothering and controlling and abusive. My underlying fears are of violence in the home, fear of having my freedom restricted and the impact on my daughter.

It may be helpful to say "This is not That". Yes, we need to pay attention to red flags, but we also need to be open to context.

How likely is this to happen? Well, I'm a very different person now to the girl who walked into that trap. I am physically stronger and I have some kickboxing and taekwondo skills under my belt. I have my own money, which would make it harder to trap me through financial reliance. I am generally a much stronger character and I am more confident about standing my ground than I was back then.

What if that doesn't happen? Well, I might just end up with somebody I like hanging out with, whose presence adds to our lives. And wouldn't that be a result worth the risk?

Ultra-Independence is a Trauma Response

When I read about this concept, it was as if a light went on in my brain.

I have spent years priding myself on my ability to do all the things. By myself.

Then I saw this – in a graphic on social media – and boom! Suddenly, it all made sense.

A quick Google search brought up an article by Gail Weiner. If this speaks to you the way it did to me, I strongly recommend you read it. She warns that independence can become "detrimental when a person becomes so independent that they fail to ask for help when they really need it."

When she talks about grief as a source of the trauma, she spells it out:

"Grief of the death of a loved one, can cause us to not allow anyone into our lives, the fear of them dying outweighs the joy of their company and we would rather not rely on their love or friendship."

Part of my resistance to relationships is because I cling to my independence. Having read that article and accepted it as making complete sense in my life, I started to make changes. One of the things she recommends is asking for help.

Have you ever noticed that asking people to help with something that benefits others is often easier than asking for help with something that benefits you?

My friend Sue invited me to see it differently. What if by not asking for help I was actually denying somebody the opportunity to feel useful? Or to demonstrate their love?

How about accepting help that has been offered when you haven't even asked for it?

Recently, I have made a conscious effort to accept offers of help from people. It feels strange, but it is also a huge relief not to have to be the one who figures out everything for herself all the time.

If you'd like to read more, there's a link to the article at the back of the book.

None of us is an island. Building relationships and trusting that the people who offer to help really do want you to accept it is another important step in your recovery.

Making My Space

When you're ready, get out your journal and write the question and then your answers.

1. What guilt do I still hold on to?

2. Was I doing the best I could with what I had at the time?

3. Do I forgive myself?

4. What anger for others do I still hold on to?

5. Is that anger helping me?

6. Do I forgive those people?

7. What am I afraid will happen if I make space?

8. How likely is that to happen?

9. What if that fear doesn't materialise?

10. What could my story look like?

11. Does ultra-independence sound familiar to me?

12. In what ways can I make my life easier by accepting help from others?

Part Four

Moving On

Pen to paper
Fingers to keys
Brush to canvas
It starts to release

Take a deep breath
And lungs expand
It's all okay
It's solid land

It's safe to feel
You can let go
It's time to heal
You can, and you know.

April 2021

Unicorns

As the old saying goes, as one door closes, another opens. Or maybe it's a window?

I have often said, when pressed to talk about 'meeting someone', that I cannot envisage living with someone else.

Remember my list of fears from the previous chapter? Your catalogue of fears can make you very picky, which is also a great way of ruling out virtually everybody you meet. Bear with me though, it's worth it...

I am also time poor, and juggling my existing commitments takes up all my time. I only get the occasional evening off and it would take somebody freaking amazing to make me want to give up on that one evening of self-indulgence. And how am I supposed to fit in all those hours on the phone of 'getting to know you' time?

My ideal new relationship is with somebody who is totally secure in themselves and enjoys their own company, someone with their own friends who sees me as a wonderful addition to an already great life. I want to be wanted rather than needed, I want to be appreciated and supported, I want to be an equal partner.

I'd also like it to be part time, at least for a while.

Not the commitment, but the actual time and energy investment.

My past experiences of living with men have not been conducive to me wanting to repeat them. Yes, I have done a great deal of work on myself and my belief in what and who I actually deserve, but I still have *that* frame of reference that says living with men leads to frustration and pain.

I look at friends who are my real-world embodiments of happily married and they also voice endless frustrations with their husbands for not appreciating that, on top of their careers, they carry the weight of the mental load for everything in the family. They still talk about the endless items of clothing left on the floor, the mugs left in the bathroom, the toilet left unflushed with the seat up, and so it goes on.

They voice all of this, but they also say that they can't imagine life without their husbands. Maybe it's a conditioning thing and it will happen to me eventually? I don't know and, right now, it doesn't matter. Living in the now means not worrying what your marriage will look like in ten years when you've only just met someone.

Then there are the very real time poverty issues that I live with. Yes, they are self-induced. Instead of getting a job and working for somebody else for a given number of hours five days a week, I have chosen to be self-employed. I have chosen not to put my daughter in daily wraparound care. I have chosen to build a business around and for her, which is great, but I currently work around fifty hours each week by getting her to bed at eight in the evening and then throwing myself into courses, calls and content creation.

Where would this new relationship fit into my already bursting-at-the-seams life?

My ideal guy works away somewhere and comes to visit once or twice a month, engaging in some kind of family activity in the daylight and ravishing me senseless at night. He understands, accepts and positively welcomes the fact that he is free to live his own life most of the time and that, while I'm good with a few texts or gifs being shared through the week, I'll only make time to speak to him properly once a week.

He is equally happy having a deep conversation or joining me for a *Star Wars* marathon. He is probably a unicorn, but that's why he's an 'ideal'. The trick is to find someone in the real world who ticks enough of those boxes.

Tony Robbins and the Ideal Partner

Several years ago, my parents very kindly let me use their timeshare apartment to go away for a fortnight in the sun. I chose to go away by myself, and it was one of the best things I have ever done. A year or two before that, I had become entranced by an infomercial for Tony Robbins and his *Get the Edge* programme. I had enthusiastically bought the pack of CDs, but struggled to sit down and listen to them. This holiday was my opportunity to do a deep self-development retreat. I had copied the entire box of CDs to my iPod and diligently packed the workbook. I lay on a sunbed on the apartment's balcony listening to a workshop each day, before going down to the pool. I wish I could say I'd taken it all on board at the time, but I think you have to be ready to change to really hear the messages!

The one workshop that really affected me, however, was the one about relationships. I have gone on to use my version of it with a number of friends. I intend to go back and listen to it again soon, but I figure you remember the bits you're supposed to remember, because they are the bits you both need and are ready for.

In the workshop, Tony asked you to write down a description of the attributes of your ideal partner. It could be anything from how they look, speak or behave, their education or income, and so on. Then you had to choose your non-negotiable attributes. On a new page, you then had to write down the things you don't want your partner to be or to have and, again, circle your non-negotiables.

At this point, you feel pretty good about how amazing and sorted your new person is going to be. Then Tony asks you to visualise that person with all of their perfect attributes. Again, it's all good.

Then he asks you to think about who *that* person's ideal partner is. Erm...

How closely do you resemble their ideal partner? Awkward...

How willing are you to change? How much do you really want that ideal partner? How much are you willing to do to be the person that your ideal partner wants to be with?

This was where I had the option of making a huge list and a massively unrealistic timetable of getting up at 4am to work out for two hours, hand milk a bunch of almonds, drink wheatgrass juice and study for an MBA, all before going to work. You get the picture.

I actually did make the list, and the timetable, many times over.

But did I do any of those things to carve my body into somebody else's ideal? Did I suddenly become financially astute? I did not.

Instead, I dropped my standards to be with people who weren't striving either.

I'm never doing that again. I'd rather be unpartnered for the rest of my days than invest myself in something or somebody that doesn't make me want to keep showing up better than before.

Kissing Frogs

I have tried to meet people over the years. I met someone when Tilly was two or three years old who I really liked. We had a lot in common, but I didn't *feel* anything. It would have been fine if he hadn't seemed keen, because I think we could have been great friends, but I didn't want to be unfair to him by spending time together while I tried to see if I was capable of having a feeling. Then I met someone who was more my type physically, but we struggled to make conversation. I came to the conclusion that I probably wasn't ready.

After several years of avoiding the issue, I tried again. The website emailed me every time somebody looked at my profile, and this one man had looked at my profile about five times a day for several days. I went to check him out and he was a police officer. As one of my friends is married to a policeman, I asked her to ask him to subtly find out whether this guy might be a suitable match or not. Subtlety was probably not my friend's husband's forte! I ended up going for a cup of tea with this guy to find out one way or another if there was any potential. His opener was, "So, tell me about yourself." I felt as if I was in a job interview. However, this paled in comparison to his second question: "How useful is your ex with childcare?"

I nearly spat my tea across the room.

My profile, the one he'd visited all those times, had my name, age and widow status beside my photo. I thought powers of observation were pretty key to being a police officer.

"Well, given that he's dead, not that useful," was my reply.

I was aghast.

I was curious to find out just how Mr Wrong the guy was. He didn't disappoint. He loved talking about himself. He was negative about the time he spent with people with mental health issues. He clearly thought he was the catch of the county.

It was enough to put me off trying again for years.

I wish I could say I was holding out for a hero, as Bonnie Tyler had encouraged me to do as a young girl, but that would be a lie. Even if that perfect knight on the fiery steed had shown up at my door at that time in my life I'd have hunted for his flaws and told him to go away. I didn't know what I wanted, but it definitely wasn't what was on offer.

Cleaver and Darcy

I will never forget being in the flat in London with Oliver in the run up to Christmas 2010, watching *Bridget Jones' Diary* on TV. "I love this movie," he said, "I always think of you when it's on." He smiled, his eyes crinkling up in the corners with a touch of lasciviousness as his eyebrow raised and he looked at the screen. Bridget was in the bunny costume for the 'Tarts and Vicars' party that had been changed to a smart garden party without anyone telling her.

I have always related to Bridget Jones – from crying with laughter on the Tube when I read the book back in 1996 to watching all the movies. I had often asked myself who were the men in my life who would fight over me. Oliver was always one of them, but I could never quite decide which one he was.

"I wish I could be your Mr Darcy baby, but we both know I'm the other guy," he said. There was no intonation or facial expression fishing for me to refute it, and the best I could come up with was, "You could try harder," and he laughed and hugged me.

He had bought a humongous television in the weeks running up to the royal wedding of Wills and Kate. He used to tell me, and anyone else who would listen, that Prince William should have married me instead. I would run through all the reasons why that was ridiculous, and then he would smile knowingly and say, "You should be with someone so much more than me." I would sometimes laugh it off, or tell him to shut up. But one day, I asked him "More *what* than you?" I was curious about who *he* thought my ideal partner should be.

"Someone who can love you properly," he said. "Someone who isn't chronically fucked up without hope of ever being normal.

"Somebody who knows how to be in a proper family, who can be a good husband and look after you.

"Somebody you can be proud of and never have to make excuses for.

"Somebody your friends really like and don't just tolerate because they love you.

"Somebody who fucking deserves you."

I cried onto his shoulder while he hugged me tightly.

"Don't waste your life crying over me when I'm gone. Be happy. Find your Mark Darcy, let him find you. Please? Promise me?"

When he started talking about dying, I would start to sing over him, or beg him to stop. Then he'd hold my face and kiss me until my knees gave way and the subject would be put away, until the next time.

A month or so after Oliver died, his father was on the phone telling me much the same thing. He told me how none of the family wanted me to waste my life in mourning and they all hoped I'd meet someone and have more children.

The thing is, when you're still with that person, no matter how excruciatingly fucking painful some of those days are, you're still with them. The thought of being with someone else is abhorrent. I was still with Oliver in the months after he left. I was still with Oliver in the months after he died. A piece of my heart will always belong to him, but I am no longer with him.

If I choose to, I am now free to be with someone else.

My Ideal Partner

When you are ready, get out your journal. Write down the questions and your answers.

1. What are the attributes I want to see in my ideal partner?

2. What are my five non-negotiables?

3. What are the attributes I don't want to see in my ideal partner?

4. What are my five non-negotiables?

5. I am focussing on my ideal partner and can see them,

hear their voice, almost touch them. Who is my ideal partner's ideal partner? What are their attributes?

6. How closely do I resemble that person?

7. If we are not one and the same, what am I willing to change?

New Beginnings

"Be careful what you wish for, you might get it"
Oliver Lund, paraphrasing Aesop

My neighbour Zoe is a big believer in manifesting. It has taken me a long time to come around to the idea that we can order what we desire from the universe, but it would seem that by constantly discussing the specifics of what a man would have to be and what he would have to be happy to accept in order to fit me, I may have done just that.

In the process of writing this book, I have processed and released so much of what has been clouding my vision that it is as if I am now wearing glasses for the first time. I am not sure if I am aware of *more*, or simply aware of *different*. What I mean is that I am seeing and feeling things I would not have noticed before, and I am not sure if that is because my eyes and my heart are opening wider or if it is because I have simply shifted my focus.

This book is finished, but I have enjoyed the therapeutic work of writing it so much that I will endeavour to continue writing about my journey and my feelings, whether I choose to share that writing or not.

June 2019

Last night, I went to a military summer ball with my best friend. As I dropped Tilly off at my parents' house before driving to Lincolnshire, I had declared my intention to kiss somebody. I made the same declaration to my friend when we arrived at the ball.

"I am going to kiss someone tonight."

She seemed pleased to hear that I was finally proactively open to meeting somebody, possibly because she had, in fact, lined up a potential new friend for me.

The evening was warm and bright and circus-themed. A big top stood on the grass outside the officers' mess and, beyond the refreshment booths, there were dodgems. Men in uniform – mostly blue but with the odd black or white – and ladies in dresses of all colours and varieties milled about, smiling and greeting each other.

Before I knew it, I was being introduced to a handsome chap called Toby. Whether he'd been briefed about me or not remains unclear, but as a first foray into dating after years of celibacy, he looked like a pretty good option.

He lives on the base in Lincolnshire so, from where I live in the West Country (a four-hour drive assuming no roadworks or incidents involving caravans), there's no immediate risk of feeling smothered and little risk of that special awkwardness when you bump into somebody repeatedly after you realise you're not a fit for each other.

He also visits his son every couple of weeks in a city less than an hour further south than us. So, if we should choose to pursue it, I could have my once or twice a month visits without it being an issue, because it already fits his life.

Do I need to plan out a life with him right now? Nope.

Whether he turns out to be my next soulmate or not is irrelevant right now. What matters is that I have tested the doors and windows and the one behind me is shut. So very thoroughly closed, in fact, that it may as well be painted shut. I'll never plaster over it, because it is part of my house, but I can redecorate it now if I want to, or leave it as is. Resting my back against it, I have a houseful of open doors and windows to choose from.

It takes time, and it takes some work, but it gets better if you let it, I promise. xx

31 October 2019

It's Halloween 2019. The day before the eighth anniversary of Oliver's death.

My eyes hurt from lack of sleep and from crying.

My back hurts. Did you know that you can cry so much and so hard that you can put your back out? Apparently, I've forgotten that I've done this before. I've forgotten because this day each year is when I drop my guard and everything is a blur and I remember him and the lives we might have led, and the here and now is not at the front of my mind.

New memories can only be made when we are fully present. I struggle to be present on these days, and why would I want to remember them? The ugly crying, the spikiness, the unpredictable emotional rollercoaster – none of it is fun. The writing is definitely helping, my laptop becoming an anchor with a long chain that allows me to safely travel backwards and forwards through time.

Last night, I opened up to one of my best friends. She knows me and knows the darkness that can creep into the shadows. She reminded me that it's okay to not be okay. She reminded me that I can be sad about Oliver and happy about my new boyfriend at the same time. She reminded me that it's okay to feel uncomfortable for a change, because it is when we step outside our comfort zone that the magic happens.

Growth and healing are not comfortable. When you've got a cut and it is healing, it itches. When you're growing taller, you ache. Your growth and healing may feel painfully slow to you, on the inside of your skin and the inside of the shadowy recesses of your mind, so slow that it is sometimes imperceptible. This is where the friends, the acquaintances who are brave enough to speak of it, come in. They have seen you change over time because they do not see you every day. They see you develop and grow and heal over time and occasionally they remind you of how far you have come.

I have come a long way. I know I have. I wish he could have too, but that was not his path.

Eight years ago today, he was still breathing.

Eight years ago today, I could have broken that ultimatum and picked up the phone.

Eight years ago today, I had that option.

Eight years ago today, I made the choice *again* to trust the professionals, who told me that having reached the point of issuing the ultimatum, I couldn't go back on it.

If I went back on it, I was signing his death warrant, because it could never be used again. He would never see me threatening to leave as anything but empty words. I had said to him so many times before that the only options were recovery or death. There was no third option.

He would never see my words as empty. He would just never see me again.

I think this is part of why I struggle so much more today, the day before the anniversary, than on the day itself. Today is the anniversary of the last chance I might have had to change things.

We would never have grown old together – growing old was never on the cards for Oliver.

We would never have had the perfect clothing catalogue family life that may or may not be attached to my vision board.

We would never have been free of his past, and he probably would have continued to have affairs.

None of that would change. But maybe, just maybe, I could have changed how I felt when he was gone. Maybe our last words to each other could have been "I love you". Or at least mine could have been.

Maybe I could have changed that single detail.

Maybe my new man is a chance to do everything better, so that I am never left with this particular sadness again. It is sometimes hard to reconcile the way he is all the things Oliver said he should be. He comes from a close family that, from what he says, genuinely like and support each other.

He likes my brother, Melissa and Colin and has quickly found common ground with them upon which to build. He looks a lot like he is falling under Tilly's spell and will love my daughter. He looks at me like I'm Christmas morning. Even when he arrives early and I haven't yet had a shower, when my hair is dirty and my house looks like a vacuum cleaner exploded in it, he looks at me like that.

It makes me wonder if maybe, just maybe, the darkness has had enough of me, at least for a while.

I cried last night. I cried with my friend, and when I went to bed, I knew I needed to open the gate. David Gray's *Babylon* was the latch. That song will forever remind me of the stretch of road around Clapham Common and Wandsworth Common. Always on our way out of London. Always full of traffic lights. When he was driving, I would look over at his profile and marvel at him being there with me. I had lived in London before I met him and it was much more my place than his. He had come there to be with me, such a reversal of our previous dynamic when I was always going to him. When I was driving, he would reach over and put his hand on my thigh. We would sing, get the words wrong, but carry on regardless.

Then I sobbed through *Please Forgive Me* and *This Year's Love* before I moved on to Adele, George Michael and Evanescence.

I am saving the big guns for tonight – Snow Patrol, James Blunt, Katy Perry, Celine and Whitney.

I had that awkward moment in the car this weekend when *Chasing Cars* played on the radio and I automatically started singing along with Toby beside me. We had another awkward moment when I cocked up the tea round and he offered to drink the cup I'd made for Melissa (but wrecked with real milk) and I squeaked, "It's an Oliver mug," because it was too weird for me.

Too weird for me to see my new man holding Oliver's mug.

A few times over the weekend, Toby asked me if I was freaking out. Mostly I said I was fine. The past couple of days I have definitely been freaking out a bit. Last night I freaked out a lot.

What if the 'making space' I was doing by 'letting go' of yet more of my internal stuff was not the right thing? What if Toby's not the right person? Please, baby, give me a sign.

And then this morning, I dropped Tilly off at school and swung by my parents to check up on them. They seemed surprised that I was still sad. It made me wonder if they thought that a new man on the scene meant I wouldn't be sad any more? And it made me question even more whether I could have any feelings for the new man while I still felt so much pain about the old one...

I reversed into our drive and had to stop suddenly. I looked into the passenger footwell. Toby's watch.

Okay.

I can take that as a sign.

He dropped it over the weekend and we both looked for it, including under the seat. We couldn't find it. And now, when I really need a sign, there it is.

Then I remember that, all week, I'd had a feeling that Oliver was listening. There was a roof leak in the building I manage and I looked at the mess behind the suspended ceiling and thought, "If only I could talk to our old electrician to ask if it was like this before." A few hours later, I bumped into him. I hadn't seen him or been able to reach him by phone for over a year.

I've had the intro to a song in my head. And guess what's playing in the car on our way home, but that very same song. Two in one day has made me wonder what the third thing will be because, if there's two, there's usually a third, right?

Whether it is Oliver, or the universe, or Neo from *The Matrix* or someone else, I am grateful for the guidance and reassurance these little moments provide. They remind me of the kind skiers who stuck out a pole to redirect my human bobsleigh away from the cliff edge.

Not all days are new territory.

You find a groove and you revisit it and find a comfort in its edges, its rails that allow you to coast on autopilot as you continue the cycle of getting up and washing your face and putting your clothes on and feeding your kids and animals and going to work and doing bedtime routines and all of the other things that fall into the comfort of a routine day. No day is entirely the same, but each day is so much easier when you have that groove to follow. You can put your energy into the moments that happen above and beyond the mundane, because the mundane happens without you needing to think about it.

Other days are filled with firsts.

Recently, I have had a lot of those.

Mostly, they are very happy firsts, but they all need to be processed. It doesn't feel as easy as some people on the outside seem to believe it should be.

I am being happy when he is dead.

I am watching another man love his child.

I am watching my child begin to love another man.

I am having mind-blowing sex with another man.

And then there are all of the bits that have nothing to do with Oliver.

I was just getting my life into the shape I wanted it to be, with me and Tilly as a team of two.

Two plus two, if you count the dogs.

Now I must process that it might be very different.

The processing is exhausting. But it's necessary. It is a vital part of the healing, like the layers of skin knitting back together after you've gashed your leg on something sharp and jagged. It may hurt, it may itch, you may want to pick it open over and over again, but it will keep trying to heal and you must let the process happen. It can't be rushed. Sometimes it needs to be covered, and sometimes it needs to be open to the air.

With light comes shade. As the sun moves and transforms your shadow from short to tall, fat to thin, left to right and front to back, you hardly notice it happening. You are busy rushing from one thing to the next and then you are in a supermarket carpark with a child who says, "Mummy, look how long our legs are!" and you pause and look down and see the shape of your shadow. The shadow that is of just you, meaning the sunlight has travelled all the way through space to the ground and you are the only thing to cross its path, right at the end of its journey.

I've always thought that's quite cool.

They will always be there as part of us, for none of us is Peter Pan, but they will change shape, size and depth with every interaction with the light.

Sunlight for the physical shadows, our light for the shadows within us.

Sometimes, you don't have a choice about what stands between you and the sun, but you have more choice about what stands between your light and the rest of the world than you might think.

There will always be hard days, tough days and some really epic level shit days in life. Without them, you wouldn't be able to appreciate the good ones.

Learning to sit in them, in the knowledge that this too shall pass, and embracing them as lessons, eases their passage through us, or maybe our passage through them.

The healing and growing is probably never 'done', but it gets better if you let it. I promise. xx

Your Happily Ever After is Unwritten

The Bedingfields played a huge part in the soundtrack of our interwoven lives. Oliver used to love arriving at my house, in a quiet development on the outskirts of Basingstoke, with his car stereo blaring. My neighbours did not love this habit, as he usually arrived after they'd put their little boy to bed. I'd be torn between delight at him singing the words at me and mortification that I would have to face justifiably grumpy neighbours, again.

On those occasions, he mostly used to play Daniel's *If You're Not The One* or Natasha's *These Words*. Both those songs have special places in my heart, but Natasha's masterpiece *Unwritten* is my favourite. It speaks to me of throwing open the windows of your life to let fresh energy in, of leaving behind whatever has happened before and embracing every possibility that being alive bestows upon you.

This is exactly what stepping out of the shadows feels like, or at least it did for me.

I still have all of the responsibilities of lone parenting. I still have all of the responsibilities of running businesses. I still live in the same house. Toby and I parted amicably about a year after we first met at that ball. The outward stuff isn't where the real magic happens.

The real life-changing magic is what happens on the inside.

It happens when you make a decision to let go of the guilt, stop punishing yourself and allow your life to get better.

I wish I could offer a magic wand to take away the pain you are feeling, but the only way to go through grief and come out the other side is to go through it.

The process, the journey of feeling the feelings and thanking them and letting them go, is what frees us.

Life is a series of moments, and every moment holds a choice.

Choose forgiveness. Choose freedom. Choose the light. Choose your life.

It gets better if you let it, I promise.

I hope reading this has helped you as much as writing it has helped me. My dearest wish is that it will help people in a situation like mine to not feel alone, and that maybe giving it to loved ones to read will help your support network to understand why you are struggling.

Grief is a many-layered rite of passage, and I believe it is something we are supposed to move through, grow through and come out the other side of. Yes, it is something we will live with for the rest of our lives, but it does not need to be a cloud that obscures the light.

I spoke to somebody while I was in the early stages of writing this and she asked me what the book was about. I had been wrestling with its purpose and what I was trying to achieve, because I knew it would only really make sense if it was raw and I was brutally honest and that meant laying myself wide open with my most vulnerable bits out there in the world.

What I heard myself say was, "You get to a point where you don't know how much you're suffering, until you're not suffering any more. If I'd known in the days of tears in the darkness that I could feel like this again, it might have made that slightly easier to bear."

Sharing your truth is a vital part of moving forward. As I learned from the *Shawshank Redemption*, the truth will set you free, but it also enables others to identify with you and release the toxic guilt and shame of their own stories.

I wholeheartedly encourage you to share your truth.

If you don't feel you can share with a friend or a loved one, you may prefer to see a counsellor and share your truth with them.

If you would like to share it with me, look me up at www.griefwithoutguilt.com

Acknowledgements

I am so blessed and so grateful.

My beautiful Tilly. Thank you for giving me a reason to keep breathing when I needed one. For bringing me so much joy and laughter that I struggle sometimes to remember what it was like before. For inviting me always to see the world through your unblinkered eyes. For being the catalyst for so many of my friendships. For giving me my first ever hometown. For encouraging me to be the best version of me that I can be and for being a source of endless pure love.

My parents. Thank you for your unflinching support through some of the darkest days of my life. I am not sure I'd have made it out without you. My beautiful daughter gave me a reason to get out of bed, to eat, to leave the house, to interact with other humans. You gave me a safe place to exist in, fed me nourishing food, cuddled me, gave me space, stepped in to rock my baby when I just couldn't function any more in the middle of the night, and have continued to backstop my life.

My brother for forgiving me.

Melissa for forgiving me, for loving us, for never shying away from remembering Oliver as he truly was and being the little sister I always wanted.

Colin. There just aren't words, mate. And if I go first, you are doing my eulogy, because I want laughs. So there.

My wider family and family friends who may as well be blood, for consistently showing up.

My friends – the family I have chosen. Sara, Kat, Jo, Amy, Charlotte, Carry… I have mentioned but a handful of you by name in these pages, but I hope you all know how much I appreciate you.

Sara, because the version you saw apparently wasn't gushing enough ha ha… I love you. You're my bestie from the Welsh Westie, my beloved unpeelable orange, the keeper of my secrets and the best partner in crime I could hope for. You have never stepped back when I have needed you. I will always be glad I scared you by inviting you for a cuppa at the Union bar. Thank you for the laughs, the memories we share and the ones we are yet to make.

My oldest friends, my uni friends, my London friends, my AA friends, my NCT friends, my baby group friends, my BBs, my TAWNies, my damn-I'm-glad-I-met you friends. Thank you for reminding me of who I am, for letting me cry, for making me laugh and for lifting me up.

Cameron, whose belief in me paved the way for my life as a business owner. Thank you for always helping me believe in myself. Thank you for all of the advice and support. Thank you for telling me that writing this was a good idea.

Stewart, for being the most patient mentor I could have hoped for.

Nina, for showing me there really is no fucking excuse for not writing a book the world needs to read.

Jessica Killingley, Bookwitch extraordinaire, for believing in this book from the first day I dropped it into a group chat about business books. Thank you for *Bookcamp: Like bootcamp but with biscuits not burpees*, for, without it, I may never have actually written a word.

My Rockstar Writers Academy buddies who have helped so much with getting the concept nailed and the edits done. Special mentions to Sue Tappenden, Natalia Komis, Dr Kathrine, Cath Nolan, Ingrid, Cindy Charest, Jessica Silva, Carolina Mountford and Cathy Wassell.

My editor, Martina, for your comments and suggestions that have improved the manuscript. I hope to meet you in person at some stage, as I think we'd get on!

Eleanor Hardiman, who designed the perfect cover for my book. Oliver loved sunsets – you did him proud.

Zoe Appleby, for being my oasis of calm for a decade and for making my diagram look considerably better.

My pre-readers – Sue, Ann, Nina and Caroline – thank you so much for your time, energy, input and sanity. This book wouldn't have made it without you.

Linda Manaena, Sam Colclough and Vic Harrison for coaching me through my fear of visibility so that I was able to finish this and share it.

Ben, who heard me and accepted my truth. May your life be always happier than it was when we met.

To all who have come before me, and written or spoken words that now flow from me and I don't know if they come from the Universe or from someone else. I have tried to attribute wherever possible and apologise if I've missed anybody.

And, finally, to Oliver, who was my lover and my friend.

Other Sources of Support

Other books and authors I have mentioned and recommend include:

Sarah Knight – *The Life Changing Magic of Not giving A F*ck*

Russell Brand – *Recovery*

Brène Brown – her TED talks, books and blog are all worth investigating

Organisations you may find helpful:

If you are grieving an addict, Al-Anon is an international sibling organisation to AA for friends and family members whose lives are affected by the addictions of others. UK weblinks www.alcoholics-anonymous.org.uk and www.al-anonuk.org.uk and there will be other country specific sites for those based elsewhere.

Cruse Bereavement Counselling. UK based www.cruse.org.uk

Suited & Booted – London based charity matching up pre-loved suits and workwear with the men who need them. www.suitedbootedcentre.org.uk

The Blog that I have followed:

The one online widow I met in the early years whose words continue to resonate with me is Michelle Steinke. When her husband died unexpectedly in a plane crash, she had a toddler and a three-year-old. There were some elements of overlap in our stories, and that was enough for me to feel I was safe to read her Facebook posts and blogs without fear of being triggered into feeling I didn't belong because my story was messy.

Michelle chose life. She chose to invest in herself and her fitness so that she felt strong enough to be both parents for her kids. She then realised her mission was to help other people with their grief by using the natural endorphins in exercise. She wrote a particularly powerful post a few years back about the widow police and not giving her card back just because she had found a new love. She is a few years further along the journey than me, and I find great wisdom in her writing. I think she's amazing and, at some stage in my life, I would love to meet her and give her the biggest hug to say thank you. If you would like to, you can find her online on various platforms by searching for her by name or One Fit Widow.

Ultra-Independence Article:

https://www.gailweiner.com/post/ultra-independence-is-a-trauma-response

Lightning Source UK Ltd.
Milton Keynes UK
UKHW010626290621
386331UK00001B/52